S0-DTA-942

the Directory of the OCCULT

Hans Holzer

Official publication of the New York Committee
for the Investigation of Paranormal Occurrences

HENRY REGNERY · COMPANY

Library of Congress Cataloging in Publication Data

Holzer, Hans W 1920-
    The directory of the occult.

    1. Occult sciences—Directories. I. Title.
BF1409.H6   133'.025'73   74-6895
ISBN 0-8092-8377-8
ISBN 0-8092-8375-1 (pbk.)

Copyright © 1974 by Hans Holzer. All rights reserved.
Published by Henry Regnery Company
180 North Michigan Avenue, Chicago, Illinois 60601
Manufactured in the United States of America
Library of Congress Catalog Card Number: 74-6895
International Standard Book Number: 0-8092-8377-8 (cloth)
                                   0-8092-8375-1 (paper)

the Directory of the OCCULT

Contents

Introduction

How to Use This Book

Ten years ago it was comparatively easy to find out whether a certain occult practitioner was honest or not, good or bad, expensive or inexpensive—all one had to do was consult the person in question. It was just as easy to get a listing of the reputable research societies dealing with the phenomena that are now referred to as occult and psychic phenomena. The reason for this comparative ease was the small number of individuals and groups involved. To be a member of such a group meant leading a somewhat precarious existence on the edge of respectability, on the fringes of science, and definitely represented being a minority element in the population. To be interested in ESP, psychic phenomena, or astrology marked one immediately as an oddball, to some an interesting person, but to the majority, a strange one. Groups working in the field were either considered hopeless idealists, dealing largely in fantasy, or heroic pioneers trying to bring direction and order into a vast field devoid of scientific respectability, depending upon the point of view of the observer.

But all this has changed. The occult field is no longer a minuscule manifestation of unusual people. It is all at once a field capable of scientific exploration, a highly popular and much romanticized area of cultural, artistic, and religious expression, and it is, let there be no mistake, a commercial enterprise of increasing importance. Under the circumstances, it seemed to me that I should put my twenty-five years as a researcher in the field to some practical use for the benefit of both layman and researcher. Some sort of overview of the entire field, containing proper evaluation as well, seemed to me to be of great practical value. This became more urgent as I began to notice the infiltration into the field of fringe elements devoid of high standards, or any standards at all, thus creating even greater confusion in the minds of people with vast prejudices against the entire field. To sift the good from the bad, to point out the pitfalls, and to mark the deserving seemed equally as important as supplying information concerning the activities and the locations of all those active in the field.

There is no attempt made here to list each and every group or individual working in any given area. To the contrary, the directory addresses itself only to those considered worthy of attention, and at the same time establishes a descending list of evaluations. To do this, much research had to be done, and many factors had to be weighed. But, in the final analysis, personal judgment also entered the picture, and the responsibility for the decision concerning such listings and the "ratings" given individual practitioners or groups is essentially mine, backed by long years of experience and knowledge of the field.

Absence from these pages does not necessarily denote negative qualities for those not listed, but it may indicate the relative lack of importance of such individuals or groups; in some cases, of course, omissions are simply due to an oversight or the imperfection of my surveying activities. On the other hand, listing in these pages does not imply qualities other than those clearly stated with those listings, nor is there any personal endorsement implied. Data are, to the best of my knowledge, as up to date as they can be, considering that it takes close to a year to publish a book. From time to time, new editions of this directory will be published, bringing the material up to date and supplying additional information, when necessary.

The occult field has been divided into the subdivisions most commonly encountered, allowing the reader to look for the desired type of service or activity without having to wade through long alphabetical listings. All listings are geographical, by regions, but the index supplies a purely alphabetical listing at the back of the book. Within the geographical listings, however, no attempt has been made to use either the alphabetical approach or the merit sequence. Groups and individuals are listed in the order in which they have come to the attention of this author; thus, a highly rated listing may be followed by a low rated entry, and vice versa. Those using the directory in order to find a suitable psychic practitioner or group will naturally look in their immediate neighborhood first, travel being as difficult as it is nowadays; however, it may well be that the best known and highest rated individual practitioners are also the most sought after, making waiting a necessary evil. It is therefore recommended that the reader consider some of the lesser known individuals whose services might be readily available, so long as their ratings are on a desirable level. After all, if we do not train and employ a younger generation of professionals in the occult field, there will be no occult practitioners left twenty or thirty years hence. In this respect, the public is as responsible for the proper development of top-notch occult professionals as are the professionals themselves.

Finally, not every individual or group listed in these pages will be happy with the way in which they are described, or with the rating I have chosen to give them; if that be so, let it be remembered that my primary responsibility is not to those listed in these pages but to the public that reads and uses this book. For them, and for my own self, I must state the facts as I find them, speak the truth as I see it, whether or not it coincides with the facts or the truth as the individuals concerned see it for themselves. The directory carries no advertising, nor are listings available to individuals or groups merely by requesting them. All selections are the result of careful studies, and are at the option of the author alone.

Professor Hans Holzer
Parapsychologist, Research Director, The New York Committee for the Investigation of Paranormal Occurrences, New York.

1

The Occult Scene Today

Occult doesn't mean dark or secret, it means hidden. The hidden meaning of life, hidden implications of natural phenomena, hidden faculties in man, that is, hidden from his conscious knowledge, are all subjects for occult studies. Certain words take on false meanings, partially because they are mistranslated, partially because of popular superstitions. Witchcraft, for instance, is one of those words, conjuring up evil and old ladies on broomsticks. In fact, the word *witchcraft* means nothing more than "craft of the wise," and refers to an old religion based upon an intimate knowledge of nature. Occultism, the occult, has also taken on an ominous meaning in the mind of those who do not understand it. Some religious practitioners warn against it; fanatics see occult practices as tantamount to worshipping the devil; medical doctors sometimes think that delving into occult knowledge is the same as fantasizing, or, worse, creating negative forces; and scientists, in many instances, believe that the occult is simply nonexistent, or at any rate, exists only in the imagination of those who practice it. But the fact is, the occult sciences are a legitimate quest for hidden and deeper meanings in all aspects of nature, just as legitimate as any other scientific inquiry, but made much more difficult because they involve emotional and personal, and therefore subjective, experience. As time goes on, the boundaries between occult science and orthodox science will become more and more indistinct, one will borrow from the other until both melt into one large body of inquiry. On the other end of the spectrum, the boundaries between occult practices and religion may well become weaker, and religious experience and occult practice may become intertwined, both drawing, as they do, on the emotional element in man.

Perhaps occult is the wrong word: esoteric science, a term used with increasing frequency today, better describes what I'm talking about. In essence, I am referring to methodical, quasi-scientific inquiries into areas of human consciousness that up to now have been regarded as outside the pale of science, but that are in fact very much part of science, when man is taken as a whole, and allowances are made for a non-physical element in his makeup. Then the nineteenth-century concept of a materialistic man, consisting of less than a dollar's worth of chemicals and nothing else, falls by the wayside, and what emerges is a duality of personality, presenting both material and nonmaterial aspects, but ultimately, composed of one single life force manifested in varying degrees, densities, and forms. The opposite of esoteric is exoteric, meaning that which is outside, on the surface, readily visible. The physical body is an exoteric manifestation of human life; the spirit, the soul, the psi factor, depending upon the nomenclature you prefer, is a manifestation of the esoteric in man. To the esoterically oriented researcher, the seed of personality itself lies in the esoteric part of man, leaving the exoteric as a kind of outer shield, devoid of decision-making capabilities, and dissolved at the time of physical death without detriment to the esoteric, inner layer of consciousness that continues to function in the next dimension.

From the dawn of man, the occult element has been in existence. At first, it was called magic and seemed beyond logical explanation. Because it was fraught with dangers, it was left in the hands of the anointed priest, the shaman, who served as intermediary between man and the diety. In this early stage, the occult formed part of religion, and everything was possible, since the rational laws of nature had not yet been understood and the universe seemed governed by the whim of superior forces. During the historical development of man, religion and the occult slowly separated, one becoming a political force, the other going underground and more and more falling into the hands of special interests, while religion was for the masses. But as religion became an instrument of state politics and was frequently abused in quests for power, the carriers of the occult traditions also considered their superior knowledge of nature a weapon to be used at the proper time and place. The two establishments began to polarize, until they could no longer be reconciled.

As the original driving force in religious experience passed from the desire for illumination to the quest for power and popular acceptance, so the original meaning of occult knowledge gradually drifted from the desire for understanding of the inner workings of nature to the power to manipulate her forces. In the process, neither religion nor the occult gained deeper knowledge, but in giving up the pathway to the deepest level of revelation, they gained on the practical level. It is a moot question to determine which is more desirable—it happened that way, whether by fate or man's design, and only now do occultists realize what they have lost and try to regain it.

Today's renewed interest in the occult in all its manifestations is not so much the result of a quest for greater knowledge as the reaction against the failure of the materialistic establishment to deliver the goods. The nineteenth century promised us great advances in this century, but the technological gains have led to greater means of destruction and left us spiritually empty. Thus, increasing numbers of people turned away from the rational establishment and sought their salvation in the emotional, beyond time and space, where magic is the key that may yet unlock hidden doors inaccessible to the technician.

What makes a person turn to an occult practice or practitioner? There are those who have a genuine interest based upon revelations, the proper background, or perhaps a talent considered part of the occult scene, and they wish to learn more about it. There are those who are disillusioned with their lives, either on a material plane or on an emotional one, or who find the predictability of a rationally oriented society depressing and counter-productive in terms of enthusiasm. To regain the enthusiasm of life, they seek solutions in other areas, and the occult promises to deliver both irrationally and personally, that is, on a direct level without a necessary intermediary. These are attractive conditions, and many a dropout in society finds that he can be very much "in" where esoteric standards prevail. Many turn to occult practices and practitioners because of religious needs that have been unfulfilled by conventional churches, while still others derive erotic satisfaction from the mysteries and from certain cultist practices playing upon the hidden sexuality in religious experience. Finally, there are those who seek the occult because they accept its threatening reputation, false though it may be. It is that very threat that attracts them and gives them the aura of invincibility, a feeling of being outside society and, in many cases, the only thing that lifts them above the commonplace. Such individuals are generally satisfied with talking about the occult, or reading books dealing with it, and seldom progress to activities in the field, as they are generally incapable of a balanced approach to its many facets.

The occult field, to me, encompasses all of that which pertains to the nature of man and the universe in which he lives, but that is not covered by conventional science, religion, and philosophy. The hidden nature of man and his universe, the inner connections that link all that is and all that happens together in a system that does not allow for coincidence, accident, or imperfection, cannot be fully understood on the basis of conventional knowledge, but it becomes completely clear when measured on the occult scale. The occult approach is therefore the complement to the rational approach, and together the two roads converge into a true understanding of life.

There are three ways by which one can investigate the various phases of the occult field. The first, and most difficult still, is the purely scientific approach, relying, as it does, on outmoded tools and concepts. The second road is what I like to call the parascientific road, including the metaphysical, which explores the realms of the occult by orderly means, albeit by standards more attuned to the realities of the occult world. Finally, there is the third approach, personal and individual experience, which cannot be communicated to others in precisely the same terms as it occurs to the individual concerned, but which nevertheless is a valid experience leading to some form of illumination.

What then are the activities understood by the term "occult field." First of all, all forms of psychic phenomena, whether they be mental or physical, from ESP to parapsychology, from laboratory tests to seances, from mediumship to spontaneous experience, clairvoyance, precognition, clairaudience, clairsentience, psychometry—in short, all forms of psychic experience, everything pertaining to extraordinary abilities of the mind or the body. The occult also deals with visionary religious experience, with those elements of conventional religion that clearly indicate a direct link with dimensions other than the physical one, with cults and ritual practices of various marginal religious communities (such as witchcraft and the pagan religions), and with magic, which is understood as an intimate working knowledge of the laws of nature. But it also encompasses some rationally oriented crafts or arts not dependent upon emotional identification. These include astrology, numerology, graphology, phrenology, and palmistry, as well as such obtuse practices as the kabbalah, with its emphasis on hidden meanings in letters and numerals. Many things that modern science rejects as fitting subjects for inquiry may be nonsense or fantasy or falsehoods. However, many other subjects arbitrarily turned down by modern science are properly and excitingly dealt with by occultism, ultimately revealing enough of their inner meanings and laws to return them to the fold of science at some future date, when modern science itself has sufficiently matured to broaden its tolerance and to accept the occult findings and wisdom for its own greater benefit.

The occult covers not only groups engaged in various forms of study and inquiry, but also individuals, professional practitioners of some form of occultism, who draw upon the hidden powers of man and nature in various ways and degrees. Whether the individual practitioner of an occult phase is professional or amateur has no bearing on the outcome; the amateurs outnumber the professionals many thousand times. But for the purpose of this directory, only the professionals have been considered.

There are those who will miss the subject of UFOs, or unidentified flying objects, in these pages. Although I've heard it said that UFOs are psychic phenomena, I'm firmly convinced that they are not. The nearest the phenomenon of extraterrestrial visitation comes to the occult is the suggestion that contact between extraterrestrial visitors and humans seems to be through telepathy. But the machines themselves are physical, the visitors human-like creatures from other worlds, flesh-and-blood worlds, that is, and therefore not truly within the scope of a directory dealing with the hidden powers in man. The lore of unidentified flying objects suffers from the same general problem all aspects of the occult suffer at one time or another; inevitably, a small but noticeable number of emotionally disturbed individuals seek it out to express unfulfilled desires and frustrations. In their fantasies and unsupported claims, they create images that tend to confuse the uninitiated outsider as to the truthfulness and responsibility of the field. Thus, the individuals proclaiming loudly that they have been given rides in flying saucers to Venus or Mars, and have had discussions with beautiful Venusians in the process, without ever giving sufficient evidence for the truthfulness of such statements, are not part of the occult scene at all, but the by-product of seemingly genuine extraterrestrial communications and visitations, without, however, having the ring of truth to them. If anything, their phenomena lie in the shadowy realms of psychological maladjustments, frustrations, and wish fulfillments. However, this is merely an opinion based upon present day knowledge. It is quite impossible to prove the nonexistence of any situation conclusively, and what some such individuals fantasize about may yet come true in other instances. The responsible works by John Fuller dealing with two amazing incidents of this kind deserve serious attention. Let us recognize the presence of irresponsible and disoriented individuals among those seeking occult truths, and know the difference.

2

Scientific Establishments Dealing with the Occult

One of the most irritating questions any television or radio interviewer could ask me is what science thinks of parapsychology. This would presuppose that parapsychology was not a science and that psychic research was really outside scientific inquiry. Nothing could be further from the truth, however. To begin with, the term science itself bears some looking at. Derived from the Latin word *scire*, science does not mean total knowledge of all that is known, it means "quest for knowledge," a rational, reasonable investigative process delving into that which may be known and that which may be unknown, without prejudice, and without the need to be inflexible at any given time. It is precisely at this point that some modern scientists betray their calling. The science of the last century is not necessarily the science of today, nor is the science of today that of tomorrow. Scientific inquiry is a process that is forever changing both in structure and in values, always ready to relinquish formerly held beliefs in favor of new evidence, even if that evidence tends to make obsolete an entire body of knowledge thought to be correct at an earlier stage of scientific development.

Anyone wondering whether parapsychology and the occult sciences are properly part of science, as we understand the term in general, confuses science in general with empiric science. In empiric science there is great need for laboratory experiments with particular emphasis on repeatability of phenomena observed. This is as it should be, since the repetition of natural processes at close quarters, under competent observation and under test conditions, is of great benefit for the understanding of the processes themselves. But the fetishism of modern laboratory experiments has gone too far. When total reliability is placed only on that which is repeated at will, a large body of evidence is of necessity left outside—the phenomena loosely classed as spontaneous phenomena and experiences that happen only in nature, only once in that particular way, which cannot under any circumstances be reproduced exactly as they have originally occurred in nature. It is not possible to create the conditions under which they occurred freely under the restrictive, artificially confined conditions of the modern laboratory. A volcanic explosion, such as the eruption of Mount Aetna in Sicily, cannot possibly be reproduced in a laboratory, yet it can be observed in great detail and certain conclusions can be drawn from it. Earthquakes can be observed and measured when they do occur, but reproducing them at a comparable scale in a laboratory is out of the question.

Likewise, the incidence of psychic phenomena in the world at large is enormous and their observation quite feasible, thus assuring the scientific establishment a substantial body of evidence obtained under test conditions, that is to say, under conditions of competent observation. This large body of evidence, taken together with certain limited laboratory experiments, represents the scientific approach to parapsychology and the occult sciences. One without the other would be meaningless, and yet many orthodox scientists in this very field tend to ignore the spontaneous evidence in the field in favor of a stubborn insistence on repeatability that cannot be had; even if it could be obtained, it would only lead to false conclusions. Already there is serious doubt as to the reliability of the statistics obtained some years ago by the great pioneer in parapsychology, Dr. Joseph B. Rhine, because his subjects seem to have performed better outside the laboratory than inside in some instances. Statistics can be used to prove or disprove almost anything. If parapsychology had to rely for its scientific background on the Rhine experiments and their continuation in other schools, it would indeed be a questionable science. Happily, the body of evidence obtained from direct observation in nature is so much stronger and is being resorted to as a source of evidence by modern parapsychologists in increasing numbers.

Until thirty-five years ago, the scientific establishment took a dim view of all efforts to bring occult phenomena within the confines of organized science. Up to then, the scientific approach to the phenomena was left in the hands of the psychic research societies, which function somewhere between the metaphysical establishment and the scientific community, without, however, having the full approval or standing of a scientific body of inquiry. With the advent of Professor Rhine at Duke University, and his newly devised testing method for two forces, ESP and psi, parapsychology became a fledgling science. To be sure, Professor Rhine went to great pains to disassociate himself from all of the more complicated phenomena that might yet come under the scrutiny of the scientific establishment, not so much because he doubted them, but because he was fully aware of the difficulties ahead to be accepted into the body of science. He therefore wisely limited himself to the study of two aspects of psychic phenomena, ESP or extrasensory perception and psi or psychokinesis, the first pertaining to mental phenomena such as telepathy, the second to the study of seeming motion of inanimate objects through mental agencies. His exhaustive tests proved that man possesses a power capable of doing both of these things, and doing them under laboratory conditions. He was even able to prove that ESP and psi could be produced at will, although the results of these experiments were by no means as conclusive or spectacular as the observation of identical phenomena when they occurred unexpectedly in nature. Nevertheless, Professor Rhine represents a milestone in parapsychology in that he made the new science a child, albeit a stepchild, of the scientific establishment.

During the first years of the Rhine experiments at Duke University, there was as yet no chair in parapsychology, no doctorate, and students who wished to work with Rhine and his associates had to take other fields as majors in order to qualify for their general academic careers. Even today, some thirty years later, anyone wishing to become a doctor of parapsychology will not find a university to grant him such a degree. He may, however, study ordinary psychology and specialize in parapsychology, or he may study sociology as did Rhine and his early associate, Dr. Hornell Hart, in order to "get in" under the classical academic umbrella. But there does seem to be a different climate among academic institutions in the United States as far as parapsychology is concerned. For one thing, an increasing number of schools have established programs in the occult fields if not chairs in parapsychology, associate or assistant professorships if not full professorships, and the number of reputable academic institutions having courses in parapsychology and associated subjects runs to about a dozen at the present time. As yet there are no extensive laboratory facilities outside Duke University, but there are a number of universities allowing their resident parapsychologists the use of existing facilties. However, there is limited funding, and absolutely no government support. But there is hope and the feeling that in the years to come orthodox scientists will embrace the newly discovered truths about the nature of man.

Today, increasing numbers of teachers wish to specialize in one or the other aspects of parapsychology and are openly seeking the proper additional training. Hundreds of students write to me every month seeking entry into a school where parapsychology is being taught, with a view toward a career in this new field. As yet, the number of applicants is much larger than the facilities the academic community can offer them. Too, the employment possibilities for fully trained parapsychologists are few and hardly remunerative. But this doesn't seem to deter the youngsters asking for an opportunity to become parapsychologists or psychic researchers, and eventually the establishment will have to provide for them, one way or another.

Since parapsychology is a young science, the philosophy behind its application and research methods differs widely, depending upon the basic philosophy of the researcher in charge. For instance, Professor Hans Bender of the Freiburg, Germany, Institute of Borderline Sciences, who is negatively disposed toward the survival of human personality ideas expressed by some of his colleagues, naturally encourages all studies tending to explain psychic phenomena in a way that makes it unnecessary to assume survival beyond physical death. On the other hand, the late Professor F. J. Ducasse of Brown University, Rhode Island, a confirmed survivalist, stressed the need for additional evidence toward proof that man survived physical death in some form. The thrust of the inquiry reflects the philosophical position of those in charge, but it also reflects the climate under which the institute of learning itself must operate. When the confirmed survivalist and pioneer in reincarnation research, Dr. Ian Stevenson assumed his duties at the School of Medicine, University of Virginia, Charlottesville, he ran into a fairly hostile environment when it came to his pet subject. It is to his credit that it did not swerve him from his path of inquiry in the least. On the other hand, the majority of those associated with the University of Virginia are engaged in projects skirting the issue of survival of human personality, concentrating their efforts on ESP in living beings in its various aspects. In the United States, such an attitude is far safer than an outright survivalist stance, if a researcher wants the approval of his academic institution, of those funding it, and of the academic community at large. It is, in short, the line of least resistance, and many parapsychologists prefer to take it in order to continue with their work, rather than fighting an uphill battle toward total acceptance by an essentially hostile, materialistically inclined scientific establishment.

If I were a student looking for a career in parapsychology, I would also consider a second field of study, whether as a minor, or as a major with parapsychology as a minor. This second field should be related to parapsychology and could be psychology, sociology, literature, comparative religion, one of the technical sciences, or medicine. But in choosing a second field, the specialization that is bound to come in parapsychology as it has come in medicine will have to be considered. In other words, a parapsychologist with particular interests in statistics, or special training in electrobiology, is more likely to find employment at a research institution than a general parapsychologist would. Ultimately, scientists and technicians of many types presently working in fields that have nothing to do with parapsychology will come into the field of parapsychology, bringing their specific skills with them, but applying them to parapsychological questions and research projects, thus exploring the nature of man from totally new angles.

Today, the following aspects of parapsychology are being investigated and taught in academic institutions of learning: ESP; psychokinesis; clairvoyance; precognition; psychometry; dream interpretation; reincarnation; apparitions and auditory phenomena; telepathy; significant differences in performance under the influence of psychic stimulation; psychic and thought photography; Kirlian photography and electrobio-

logical experiments with living entities; psychic and unorthodox healing; out-of-the-body experiments (astral projec-
tions); bilocation; materialization and dematerialization;
mind and body control by purely mental means; miraculous
claims and visions involving religious and mystic experience;
the relationship between certain drugs and extension of consciousness; the human aura; color consciousness and ESP;
and other subjects that very few scientists would have believed
capable of methodical scientific exploration a scant five years
ago.

But in all fairness to those who criticize some of the unsci-
entific aspects encountered among occultists, it should be
remembered that not every metaphysician calling himself a
scientist is necessarily one. The standards that make a society,
a college, a researcher, or a scientist do include certain
minimum requirements. To begin with, such an institution
should have either a state or federal charter; that is, it should
be part of the educational scene, even if it is a private institution. Beware of some outfits calling themselves college or
Christian college or spiritual college, or some such designation, offering degrees for twenty or twenty-five dollars, by
mail of course, which have no value whatsoever. These "institutions" consist of a mail-order address and are totally
fraudulent. Unfortunately, they are legal in some states. A
charter, a staff of instructors, and a physical campus are
among the minimum requirements for an academic institution to be recognized as such. However, the interest in parapsychology need not be an extensive one, it may in fact consist
of one instructor or course. There is no need for a degree in
parapsychology, or even credit for courses given, if the classes
are in the adult education or university extension areas.
Nevertheless, the fact that they are given under the sponsor-
ship of an established institution will in most cases guarantee
the student a certain level of academic accomplishment and
reliability of information. In addition, there are a number of

private societies of quasi-academic standing, and they will be dealt with further on in this chapter.

As for the student, the minimum required is a high school diploma, although the majority of research applicants in parapsychology are at the B.A. or B.S. level. I have found a number of postgraduates interested in the field, even people with doctorates in other areas.

Every new science has had its detractors at first, only to be better understood and received into the fold of the recognized science establishment eventually. When Dr. Sigmund Freud proposed the basic tenets of psychiatry, his own colleagues in the medical establishment laughed at him, and when he persisted, became openly hostile toward him. It took psychiatry many years after Freud's initial efforts to establish it, until it was considered legitimate, and many more years before it became popularly accepted. During those early years, the popular press as well as the medical press heaped abuse on Freud, published caricatures of the discoverer of psychoanalysis, and expressed the firm conviction that Freud was wrong and his ideas would die with him. Of course, much the same thing had happened to Thomas Alva Edison and the electric light. A congress of distinguished scientists specializing in physics declared that Edison's invention, the electric bulb, would never work or become generally accepted. There were those who publicly proclaimed that the "toy" of the Wright Brothers was just that and nothing more. Man's history is filled with poor judgments on the part of established scientists or experts, and progress is being made only because some individuals are undaunted by the negative response to their discoveries or views. Similarly, the attitude displayed toward parapsychology and the occult sciences in general by the mundane press and by some of the establishment scientists, is not likely to prevent the ultimate breakthrough of that new science to much larger popular and professional levels. But it makes progress that much more difficult.

One can perhaps understand the material mailed out by the various groups in the Baptist establishment, containing such colorful headlines as "The Seance Exposed," telling the reader that God's scriptures promised punishment to those who consult the dead through mediums, claiming that scriptures denounce spiritualism (which was founded roughly nineteen hundred years after the scriptures were conceived), even stooping to attacking individual psychics such as Jeane Dixon, calling her a false prophetess because she does not prophesy in the name of the Lord Jesus Christ. This, of course, must come as a shock to Mrs. Dixon, a devout Roman Catholic who never misses an opportunity to display her religious sentiments. One can overlook this kind of childish intellecutal garbage mailed out by a church establishment that feels itself somehow threatened, and one can even laugh at such newspaper columns as Gerald Nachman's "Double Take," which proclaimed that a White House witch-hunt would be undertaken very shortly to find out what evil forces had erased the Watergate tapes. Mr. Nachman's humor has gone over the heads of many of his readers, unfortunately, for when he wrote that a panel would be convened in the White House to exorcise the sinister force at work on those tapes, including myself, Uri Geller, the Amazing Kreskin, Anton LaVey, and William Peter Blatty, several dozen people wrote to me wondering whether I had actually gone to Washington on this assignment.

But I find it a lot more destructive when a responsible major news magazine such as *Time* engages in a 1974 witch-hunt into the area of parapsychology and the occult sciences, smacking of yellow journalism of the worst kind. A pictorial report showed a device set up to record out-of-the-body experiences at the American Society for Psychical Research and was labeled "Questionable Procedures Costumed in the Prim Gown of Laboratory Respectability." Yet, fifteen years ago, the later Professor Hornell Hart of Duke University experimented with out-of-the-body experiences with some three hundred of his students, published his findings in respected scientific journals, and established the classical patterns that have long proved that such excursions are indeed possible, and, incidentally, perfectly natural and not miraculous. *Time* then went on to quote a small number of so-called authorities, of its own selection, who all happen to be hostile toward parapsychology and the occult sciences, and who also happen not to have ever worked in the field themselves, but in other areas that do not necessarily qualify them to judge the phenomena investigated by parapsychology. These include a mathematics analyst named Martin Gardner, the writer Daniel Cohen (author of a children's book on ghosts and a couple of unsuccessful collections of strange tales), a couple of magicians, Charles Reynolds and the "Amazing Randi" (who amazed me several years ago by stating that he "never read books" when I quoted some of the writings of Professor Rhine to him on a radio program). Uri Geller, probably the most amazing physical medium of the century, was attacked and his skills were derided. Yet, a professional engineer of my acquaintance has held a metal fork in his closed fist, while Geller, from some distance away, managed to bend it. Geller, of course, has performed seeming miracles in the presence of competent scientists time and again, his experiments have been filmed and photographed and analyzed, and there is no question among parapsychologists that he has an enormous amount of physical mediumship or psi power. *Time* also did not like Cleve Backster and his experiments with the sensitivity of plants.

"The work of two occult journalists, *Secret Life of Plants* is an anthology of the absurd costumed in the prim gown of laboratory respectability," writes *Time*, employing the same phrase used two pages earlier for out-of-the-body experiments at the American Society for Psychical Research—evidently running short of picturesque clichés. I am not sure I know what "an occult journalist" is, but the authors of this remarkable work on plant sensitivity are trained science writers with an impressive background in the very field they are writing about.

Perhaps the most outrageous attack upon the integrity of reputable scientists was contained in a red-bordered box labeled, "A Long History of Hoaxes," in which a picture of Professor Rhine taken in 1940 appeared with the statement, "from the start Rhine was criticized for juggling numbers," and then went on to describe Rhine's inspiration as pictures of fairies published by the late Sir Arthur Conan Doyle, "manifestly staged," as *Time* put it. Of course, the *Time* writer did not take the trouble to investigate the original material. He assumed it was all trickery. He then turned his attention to a more recent psychic photographer by the name of Ted Serios, whose thought-photography experiments have been fully investigated for several years by Dr. Jule Eisenbud and a large number of scientists at the University of Colorado and elsewhere. I have myself seen the series of photographs taken of Ted Serios showing clearly how his exteriorized thoughts gradually replace the face on the film. These were taken by Professor Bill Jeffries of the University of Bridgeport, Connecticut, who is a professor of mechanical engineering and an expert parapsychologist. Yet, *Time* classed the Serios experiments as among the hoaxes, stating "reporters Charles Reynolds and David Eisendrath, who observed Serios at work in Denver had little trouble constructing a device that could be secreted inside a gismo to produce all of Serios' effects." In other words, the fact that two photographers could fake what Serios did was to *Time* tantamount to Serios having actually faked it. By the same logic, the gun in a man's pocket automatically makes him a murderer, because he *could* use the gun to shoot someone. Ted Serios did not use trickery, he has

sent thought images into television tubes, and he has produced images of objects thousands of miles away with which
he wasn't familiar. The University of Colorado and the brilliant scientists who have spent many years investigating
thought photography with Ted Serios are not likely to pay
attention to this kind of innuendo. It is the public in need of a
balanced, unbiased overview of this exciting field that is being
defrauded by the likes of *Time* magazine. The magazine
ended its attack on the field by stating, "there is only one way
to tell, by a thorough examination of the phenomena by those
who do not express an a priori belief." But *Time* magazine
itself has expressed just that belief, or rather disbelief, that
makes it impossible for its reporters and writers to present an
accurate image of parapsychology and the occult sciences.

Fortunately for the public, other publications take a more
mature position on this vital subject. In a survey entitled
"Why Scientists Take Psychic Research Seriously," *Business
Week* stated recently, "   . . . if firmly established and
developed, psychic powers would have potential applications
in medicine, communications, defense, education, and a host
of other fields. But the greatest impact could be on mankind.
Researchers are convinced that everyone possesses some dor-
mant psychic powers that can be developed."

In the following pages, the leading scientific institutions
dealing with the field will be listed and their work and relative
standing will be discussed.

California

The Los Angeles branch of the American Society for Psychical Research owes much to the late Marjorie D. Kern, who
founded this west coast branch and maintained its activities
with the support of west coast residents interested in psychic
research and sometimes without the support of the main
office in New York. The Los Angeles branch still exists, and

forums, lectures, and investigative work continues. In recent times, an investigation by the Los Angeles branch of the American Society for Psychical Research in conjunction with Dr. Thelma Moss of U.C.L.A. into local haunted houses has drawn the attention of both press and serious researchers. The activities of this group are open to the general public. The last known address is: 1414 Club View Drive, Los Angeles, California 90024. **Recommended.**

The parapsychology team headed by Dr. Thelma Moss at U.C.L.A., University of California, Los Angeles School of Medicine, is located on the campus of this very large university in Westwood. Dr. Moss, who came to parapsychology comparatively late in life, having first been a successful Broadway actress under the name of Thelma Schee, has nevertheless caught up rapidly in her newly chosen field with the exciting innovations of scientifically investigating psychic healing, Kirlian photography, and other forms of research including field work. She teaches classes in parapsychology and is probably the best qualified psychic researcher in southern California today. **Recommended.**

Dr. Patrick Flanagan, in his early thirties, is essentially a one-man organization concentrating on what he calls biological energy research. Popularly known as the "pyramid man" because of his writings and demonstrations involving pyramid power, Dr. Flanagan explained his theories to me during a recent interview.

"I came here from Houston, Texas, and acquired a Ph.D. in physics from Mary Stewart International University, based on my biological energies research. At first I became involved in a new concept of a hearing aid called the neurophone which transmits sound by passing an impulse into the cranial nerve. The hearing aid played an important part in my discoveries, because one day I was making photographs in my darkroom when I discovered what looked like the outline of an energy aura around my finger. This had been stimulated by my neurophone which is a high-voltage transmission device. From that I became involved in Kirlian photography. Eventually I became interested in the study of pyramid power. In the 1930s a Frenchman by the name of Bovis discovered mummified animals, small rodents which had wandered into the Egyptian pyramids and starved to death and yet their bodies were mummified. Later, Czechoslovakian researchers were able to sharpen razor blades by putting them into pyramids, and I have expanded on this and discovered the basic key behind pyramid power as well as its relationship to the energies within the body."

Dr. Flanagan is the author of several books on pyramid power, and his company markets various devices designed to supply pyramid energy to the users. There is, first of all, a large plastic pyramid, large enough to sit under for the suggested periods of fifteen to thirty minutes at a time. People sitting under the pyramid tent are surrounded by energy, which is somehow concentrated or channeled by the pyramid shape. There is also a pyramid energy generator consisting of fifteen one-inch-high pyramids on a three-by-five-inch base, containing its own magnetic field source in the plastic base. This device, Dr. Flanagan says, will work in any position and within any structure, it will sharpen razor blades, remove bitterness from liquids, improve the taste of cheap wines and liquors, drastically change instant coffee, keep carrot juice from lumping, and mummify organic matter. Those wishing to study Dr. Flanagan's theories and experimental research more closely may find additional information in his pamphlet, "The Pyramid and Its Relationship to Biocosmic Energy." The address of his company is: Pyramid Products, 438 West Cypress, Glendale, California 91205. **Recommended.**

Going back in age almost to the early days of Duke University is Palo Alto's Stanford University Research Institute. The main researchers and teachers here are Dr. Russell Targ and Dr. William Tiller. The facilities are open to registered students and postgraduate researchers, and the institute publishes its findings from time to time. **Recommended.**

One of the newest research foundations dealing with parapsychology is the Noetics Foundation, dealing with what its founder and director calls "the science of consciousness," but actually it is dedicated to all aspects of psychic research. This director and founder is astronaut Dr. Edgar Mitchell. Dr. Mitchell has been quite outspoken in his conviction that psychic phenomena are real. His interest in the field received its greatest impetus from the unusual experiences he went through while an astronaut, but as a scientist he has always been fascinated by the so-called unknown. Dr. Mitchell's work as a researcher and lecturer deserves the greatest respect and support. The foundation may be addressed: care of *Psychic* magazine, 680 Beach Street, San Francisco, California 94109. **Recommended.**

Colorado

Several years ago, a bellhop in a Chicago hotel was brought to my attention by *Fate* magazine, because he possessed unusual psychic talents. However, I discovered that this man, Ted Serios, could perform most satisfactorily when somewhat inebriated. I felt that this was a hindrance and did not pursue the matter. Mr. Serios then was introduced to Dr. Jule Eisenbud of the University of Colorado, a reputable psychiatrist and parapsychologist. There ensued long years of studies under test conditions, during which Mr. Serios was able to produce satisfactory evidence of his ability to project thought images not only into cameras and onto photographic film, but also into television tubes. Naturally, the experiments came under attack from assorted magicians and photographers who mistook their own ability to duplicate Mr. Serios's feats as proof that he had used fraud in producing them in the first place. I have personally inspected photographs taken under test conditions and am satisfied that no fraud was ever involved in the experiments at the University of Colorado. Since that time and the publication of a book about *The World of Ted Serios* by Dr. Jule Eisenbud, Ted Serios has become the most sought after photography medium among scientific research groups. He has traveled from university to university, without publicity, without much remuneration, to serve as a guinea pig to those parapsychologists and other scientists open-minded enough to investigate his unusual, but by no means unique, talents. There continues today at the University of Colorado a research effort in parapsychology, undertaken by the aforementioned Dr. Jule Eisenbud. Those who wish to study there or contact Dr. Eisenbud for questions of research may do so at the University of Colorado or: 4634 East Sixth Avenue, Denver, Colorado 80220. **Recommended.**

Florida

Metapsychiatry is a term coined by Stanley R. Dean, M.D., prominent physician and researcher, graduate of the University of Michigan Medical School and a practicing psychiatrist and clinical professor of psychiatry at the University of Miami Medical School in Miami, Florida. "I have selected this term to designate the important but hitherto unclassified interface between psychiatry and mysticism," Dr. Dean states. "Metapsychiatry encompasses not only parapsychology but also all other suprasensory, suprarational, and so-called 'supernatural' manifestations of consciousness that are in any way relevant to the theory and practice of psychiatry. Sufficient proof has been established for the existence of psychic phenomena, and now the current need is to disseminate the scientific basis of such phenomena, their relevance to psychiatry, and their development for the betterment of mankind."

An article by Dr. Dean, which first appeared in the *American Journal of Psychiatry* in September of 1973, was subsequently inserted into the *Congressional Record* by the Florida representative Claude Pepper. Students, especially future medical doctors, who wish to include meta-psychiatry and the occult in their studies might do well to contact Dr. Stanley R. Dean through the University of Miami Medical School, Miami, Florida. **Recommended.**

On a decidedly different level, but just as serious in its own way, is the research effort undertaken by one of the great pioneers of reincarnation work, Morey Bernstein, the celebrated author of *The Search for Bridey Murphy.* Mr. Bernstein is a one-man organization, but he has worked with others doing worthwhile research in the field. Those interested in reincarnation research in particular might be able to contact him at: 1830 South Treasure Drive, Miami, Florida. **Recommended.**

New Jersey

The Newark College of Engineering, Newark, New Jersey, has maintained a laboratory dedicated to parapsychology for several years now, headed by E. Douglas Dean, formerly with the Parapsychology Foundation of New York. Mr. Dean teaches parapsychology, both in the laboratory and in the field, and I believe students of college level are being admitted. Those wishing to obtain details of the curriculum should contact the Newark College of Engineering directly. **Recommended.**

The Psychic Phenomena Society of New Jersey is a comparatively new organization, the result of combining several smaller groups interested in psychic research in the area. While it does not pretend to have the academic standing of a university, it is nevertheless a notch above a metaphysical group, and its standards are very high. The society is headed by George Adler and maintains a regular program of monthly lectures. It also contains a psychic information exchange, a library service, and informal talk sessions with leading researchers and sensitives in the field. Those wishing to subscribe to its newsletter or partake in its activities, should contact: Psychic Phenomena Society of New Jersey, Kingston, New Jersey 08528. **Recommended.**

The Jersey Society of Parapsychology is another research society composed mainly of interested laymen, but maintaining a high level of inquiry and arranging lectures on various phases of parapsychological research from time to time. Address: Post Office Box 2071, Morristown, New Jersey 07960. **Satisfactory.**

Drew University, Madison, New Jersey, has sponsored parapsychology seminars for several years. Although this school does not as yet maintain a year-round department of parapsychology, those interested in studying there might inquire concerning these seminars and special study periods. **Satisfactory.**

New York

The oldest and best known research body in this country is the American Society for Psychical Research, founded in 1885 as the result of a visit by Sir W. F. Barrett to America. It tried to emulate in the United States what the British Society for Psychical Research was already doing in Great Britain. Later, the American society became a branch of the British society until the death of its first president, Dr. Richard Hodgson, in 1905. At that time, the American society was reestablished as a separate entity under Dr. James H. Hyslop, formerly professor of logic and ethics at Columbia University.

The society publishes the *Journal of the American Society for Psychical Research,* a monthly publication of extremely technical scientific material. It also publishes a newsletter of more mundane contents, including listings of various group activities and lectures pertaining to the field. Nobody will ever accuse the society of being too forward or optimistic in its appraisal of the results of psychic research. To the contrary, much of the material published by the society tends to dampen the enthusiasm of some researchers, such as myself, who are firmly convinced of the reality of survival of bodily death. In this respect, the American Society for Psychical Research represents a step backward in its position, for the late-nineteenth-century researchers, especially in England, were already on firm ground when they maintained that survival had been proven. But the works of the likes of F. W. Myers and the cross-correspondences seemingly indicative of survival evidence are seldom mentioned in its pages today. What takes up a great deal of time and space in the society's efforts is dedicated to various statistical investigations, to evaluations and theorizing within the materialist concept of present day science. Whether or not one agrees with the self-imposed limits of this august society, membership in it is a must for anyone seriously interested in the field. Address: 5 West Seventy-third Street, New York, New York 10023. **Recommended.**

Parapsychology Foundation, Inc., is a foundation dedicated to the support of parapsychological research, wherever it may be undertaken. The brainchild of the late Eileen Garrett, Parapsychology Foundation was at first rather reluctant to step into the limelight of publicity, at a time when support for psychic research was not considered proper for men of science. Much of the funding of this foundation came from Ohio representative Frances Bolton, a dedicated supporter of psychic research, and the work is being carried on by Mrs. Garrett's daughter, Eileen Cooly and a staff of researchers, administrators, and librarians. Originally, Parapsychology Foundation published *Tomorrow* magazine, turning it from a general magazine into one dedicated to psychic research. When *Tomorrow* magazine had run its course, the Foundation started to publish the *International Parapsychology Review*, which in turn became just *Parapsychology Review*, which is still being published today. When Eileen Garrett was at the helm of the foundation, funds were given to deserving researchers, such as Mr. Frazer Nichol and Professor Rhine at Duke University, Andreja Puharich and his Maine roundtable conference, and to me, for the investigation of haunted houses in the eastern United States. At present, Parapsychology Foundation is not an ordinary membership society, nor does it arrange for lectures or study courses. It is a sort of roof organization or clearinghouse for other parapsychological organizations, but the library at its headquarters is open to researchers upon request. Address: 29 West Fifty-seventh Street, New York, New York 10019. Telephone: PL1-5940. **Recommended.**

A newcomer in the field is the Foundation for Parasensory Investigation. This is the organization that first brought celebrated Israeli sensitive Uri Geller to public attention in the United States. The Foundation for Parasensory Investigation sponsors lectures and study courses and attempts to combine scientific standards with popular appeal. Address: One West Eighty-first Street, Suite 5D, New York, New York. Telephone: 799-4686. **Recommended.**

Although not a full-fledged department of parapsychology, City College, New York City, does maintain an interest in psychic research in the person of Dr. Gertrude Schmeidler of the Department of Psychiatry, who has done much research and frequently lectures in this field. **Satisfactory.**

The distinguished psychiatrist Dr. Robert Laidlaw, once a close coworker of the late Eileen Garrett in the investigation of unusual cases, has recently delved into the investigation of psychic healers, both here and abroad. I am not aware of any study courses given by this distinguished researcher, but he is, or was, a leading physician in the department of psychiatry at Roosevelt Hospital, New York City. **Recommended.**

The New York Committee for the Investigation of Paranormal Occurrences is the title given by me to the small group of associates working with me over the years in the investigation of hauntings and other paranormal cases. The committee was founded in 1962 under the auspices of the Parapsychology Foundation and Eileen Garrett, in order to receive the modest study grants she wanted me to have for the investigation of certain cases in the eastern United States. The committee is a private organization and does not publish anything as such, but much of the research material obtained by the committee appears in some of my books. The committee, under my guidance, also investigates claims of mediumship and trains promising sensitives at no cost. Those wishing to report unusual paranormal cases, or substantiated evidence of mediumship, or seek relevant information in this field may address themselves by mail only to: Professor Hans Holzer, 140 Riverside Drive, New York, New York 10024.

The New York Institute of Technology has been giving courses in parapsychology as part of its adult education program for the past four years. These courses have included parapsychology one (introduction), parapsychology two (experimental) and parapsychology three (incorporating comparative religion). The classes in parapsychology are taught by Professor Hans Holzer. Address: 888 Seventh Avenue, New York, New York.

Over in Brooklyn, New York, the Maimonides Medical Center maintains a dream laboratory as part of its department of psychiatry. Headed by parapsychologist Dr. Stanley Krippner, the laboratory has been in the headlines for its valid research into REM or rapid eye movements during sleep. But the laboratory's work goes far beyond the observation of subjects while asleep, with the help of electrodes and other apparatus. Dr. Krippner delves into other areas of consciousness and the relationship between ESP and the sleep state. Those who wish to study in this area and have the proper academic qualifications, may contact the dream laboratory at: Department of Psychiatry, Maimonides Medical Center, Brooklyn, New York 11219. **Recommended.**

North Carolina

The area around Durham is the center of several psychic research bodies, not so much because of the warm climate, but because the original research center at Duke University, supported by the Duke tobacco millions, was located here. Officially called the Parapsychology Laboratory at Duke University, it was the first of its kind in the United States in the 1930s when Professor Joseph Banks Rhine and his wife Louisa began teaching the rudiments of parapsychology. Today, others have taken up the work at Duke University, but some research is still being carried on, although on a much reduced scale. Those wishing to take classes in parapsychology in conjunction with other study courses at Duke University should address the dean directly. **Recommended.**

Also at Durham, North Carolina, the independent Psychical Research Foundation headed by W. G. Roll, Danish-born researcher and author, carries on its valuable work. Mr. Roll has published some of his findings in the *Journal of the American Society* and is an active participant in the Parapsychology Association. The latter, composed of some (but not all) researchers active in parapsychology, headquarters at the University of Virginia, Charlottesville, Virginia. **Satisfactory.**

The "father of modern parapsychology," Professor J. B. Rhine, nowadays carries on his work at Chapel Hill, North Carolina, under the name of Foundation for Research on the Nature of Man. Those wishing to study at Chapel Hill may inquire as to the feasibility of taking classes with Professor Rhine. **Recommended.**

Ohio

The Parapsychology Forum of Cincinnati, established in 1970, meets twice a month for study, discussion, and experimentation. Two of the members teach ESP classes in adult education courses in the city. The group helps start new study groups when requested, provides speakers on the subject of parapsychology to local groups, investigates reports of hauntings, and assists in helping to locate missing people or objects. Members feel that psychic development, study, and sharing of experiences is best accomplished in a small group where rapport is more easily established and maintained than in a large organization where meetings tend to be lectures rather than participation. There are now three Forum study groups in Cincinnati, including an evening group, which allows those unable to attend during the day to meet with those who share a common interest.

The Forum's first president, Mrs. Virginia Cameron, an indefatigable worker for the cause, has recently relocated in Florida. The society is now in the equally able hands of Mrs. Janet Tubbs and has won the respect of the Cincinnati news media and the academic establishment. Those in the area wishing to participate in Forum activities should write to: Parapsychology Forum of Cincinnati, Post Office Box 24105, Cincinnati, Ohio 45224. **Recommended.**

Virginia

Probably the best school dealing in parapsychology today is the University of Virginia School of Medicine, Charlottesville, Virginia. Headed by Dr. Ian Stevenson and Dr. Gaither Pratt, formerly of Duke University, the school offers a reasonable curriculum in various aspects of parapsychology. Dr. Stevenson is an expert on the difficult subject of reincarnation and the author of *Twenty Cases Suggestive of Reincarnation,* which has rapidly become a classic in the field. While it was necessary for early students at Duke University to engage in the study of sociology or psychology in order to qualify for parapsychological work, this is no longer necessary at the University of Virginia where one may follow one's inclination in this respect without the need for camouflage. Those who wish to study at the University of Virginia should address themselves to Dr. Stevenson at the School of Medicine or to the dean. **Recommended.**

Canada

The Barrie Society for Psychical Research is a small but reputable group investigating psychic phenomena and arranging for lectures and classes in the field. It is headed by Mrs. Shirley D. Jones, and those living in the area of Ontario close enough to Barrie and the greater Toronto area might wish to inquire further from: Barrie Society for Psychical Research, Post Office Box 581, Ontario, Canada. **Satisfactory.**

Although not a research society as such, attention should be drawn to the activities of Sercolab, a manufacturer of tools and scientific instruments used in parapsychological research. Secrolab is headed by Dr. Harry E. Stockman, Harvard '46, and is located at: Post Office Box 78, Arlington, Massachusetts 02174. **Recommended.**

There are many other psychic research societies throughout this country and Canada, and some of them merely the result of interested laymen getting together to form groups, others connected with local colleges or speaker forums. A number of colleges are instituting courses in parapsychology or at least sessions on the subject within existing courses. I have listed and discussed here only those personally known to me and hope to include others, currently outside the scope of this book, in future editions. I am therefore grateful to anyone concerned who wishes to communicate to me pertinent information and data.

3

The Metaphysical Establishment

Metaphysics is frequently misunderstood; some people think it is a religion or group of religions, others think it has something to do with physics, while still others have a vague notion that metaphysics is the same as psychical research, parapsychology, in short a scientific effort. It is, of course, none of those things. The word *metaphysics* means that it is beyond physical law, that is, the subject matter is somehow not covered by ordinary physical law, and therefore subject to some other, different set of laws. I should like to define metaphysics as the vast area of spiritual probing and awareness that lies beyond conventional religion, but this side of scientific inquiry. The metaphysician does not attempt to prove that his beliefs are valid by laboratory experiments or by orthodox scientific methods, the way empiric science does. Metaphysics requires faith and acceptance of a spiritual universe, as different from the physical universe, although part of it. To accept metaphysics as a philosophy of life, one has to orient oneself in three directions: (1) the belief in and conviction of continuance of life beyond physical death; (2) the existence of a set of laws governing man and all living creatures, sometimes in conflict with orthodox natural law, sometimes merely beyond it, and at all times the result of some higher power, whether it be defined as God, world mind, spiritual awareness, or any number of similar designations; and (3) the belief that man can change his status and improve his position in life by following these laws and by allowing destiny to guide him into the right channels.

Today, metaphysics is a term loosely applied to just about every form of unorthodox religion, cult, and spiritual awareness endeavor, as well as to a wide range of practitioners from Spiritualist ministers to mind expansion teachers, to psychic healers, and even to ministers of minority churches who preach a gospel differing from the ordinary biblical concept, or who accept the equality of all religions as a basic tenet. Consequently, the metaphysical establishment contains some very valid people and ideas, some less valid but nevertheless harmless concepts, and also some outfits and individuals out for profit, or at the very least, wallowing in self-delusion. The latter, to be sure, are in the minority, and their teachings are frequently so obtuse that they make little sense except to themselves, but the outsider gets a slanted picture of the entire field if he accepts such groups or individuals as representative of the metaphysical approach to life.

In reporting here on the groups and individuals I have personally met, there were borderline cases where the question arose: Is this a scientifically oriented organization or is it metaphysical, relying solely on acceptance of its tenets by faith? There are some reputable organizations that pursue their quest toward enlightenment both by scientific evaluation methods and on faith. But I have said many times that belief is that which you cannot prove successfully on evidence, and have therefore classed these borderline cases as being in the metaphysical establishment.

National Organizations

Spriritual Frontiers Fellowship was founded by the late Arthur Ford and a group of concerned ministers, with the avowed purpose of creating an organization that would deal in psychic research as it applied to the ministry as well as to the layman. In one way, Spiritual Frontiers Fellowship tries to interest the church in becoming involved in psychic research, and it has done very well indeed in this area. This is in part due to the fact that many professional ministers belong to Spiritual Frontiers Fellowship and partially because of the extensive lecture and publication program the organization maintains. But Spiritual Frontiers Fellowship has also been useful to those individuals who cannot decide which direction to go in, who do not wish to commit themselves to a particular metaphysical organization or cult, and who prefer a general, middle-of-the-road approach to spirituality. Membership in the organization is possible both for groups and individuals. Main office: 800 Custer, Evanston, Illinois 60202. **Recommended.**

The Theosophical lodges, originally founded by Madame Helen Blavatsky, teach a philosophy incorporating belief in reincarnation, peaceful existence, and God consciousness without being too literal about the nature of God. Thus, Christians, Jews, Muhammedans, and other religions can freely partake of theosophical concepts without having to break with their earlier religious affiliations. Theosophy lodges exist in all major cities of the United States and can be located in telephone directories. Notable are the lodges in New York City and St. Louis, Missouri, as well as those in Los Angeles and Chicago. **Recommended.**

Anthroposophy is an offshoot of theosophy, a philosophy based upon the concepts and writings of Rudolf Steiner, and it differs somewhat from theosophy in that man becomes the center of the universe rather than the Godhead within. Although not as farflung as theosophy, anthroposophical lodges exist in many American cities, and there are also schools following the Rudolf Steiner concepts. **Recommended.**

The Association for Research and Enlightenment, popularly known as the Edgar Cayce Foundation, headquarters at Virginia Beach, Virginia, but has branches in many American cities. It is primarily a repository of the "readings" given by the late Edgar Cayce, carefully filed according to subject and available to its members. In addition, the ARE sponsors classes, lectures, and instruction courses, both at its headquarters and at its many branches. The ARE also publishes inspirational literature and many of the writings about Edgar Cayce by a variety of authors. In a way, headquarters of the foundation at Virginia Beach is a way of life and an industry at the same time. Under the direction of Cayce's son, Hugh Lynn Cayce, it runs smoothly and produces a considerable impact upon the general scene. Whereas ten years ago, only those interested in metaphysics would have known about ARE, the organization has of late frequently broken into the news, and its membership numbers many thousands. There are several classes of membership available, depending upon the desire to receive the so-called Black Book, containing the medical readings by the late Edgar Cayce, or just the newsletter and the journal, which publishes short articles and book reviews. ARE may be reached at: Post Office Box 595, Virginia Beach, Virginia 23451. Telephone: 804-428-3588. The New York group, probably the most active among the many groups, is located at: 34 West Thirty-fifth Street, New York, New York 10001. ARE is a nonprofit organization led by reputable men for a worthy cause. I think anyone interested in metaphysical ways should, at the very least, be interested in its work, if not a member. **Recommended.**

Silva Mind Control has mushroomed from a comparatively

modest layout at Laredo, Texas, several years ago to a nation-wide organization of tightly organized branches, where individuals may learn the techniques of mind control. The basic tenet of this method is the brainchild of Jose Silva, and his message, in his own words, is that "we all have psychic ability that can be cultivated to our advantage. Mind control lets you choose levels of awareness at which you want to function. You can improve the skills within your intellectual potential, such skills as concentration, memory, creative imagination, and verbal or artistic expression. You can bolster such personality components as self-confidence, motivation and leadership. You can correct such disturbing behavior patterns as excessive drinking, smoking and over-eating, nervous tension, shyness and insomnia." Essentially, Mr. Silva teaches that there are two levels of consciousness, alpha and beta levels, and it is by descending to the deeper level that man can reach psychic dimensions, even reaching out to other minds and obtaining knowledge by a method that is ordinarily not available to him. There is nothing particularly startling about the mind control ideas, and they seem to work in many instances. It stands to reason that not everyone taking Mr. Silva's classes will turn into a competent medium, or a person able to break through the time-space barrier after six easy lessons. But some do, while others merely improve their own minds, or rather the control over them. There is nothing harmful in this method, if it is looked at as simply another way of extending one's mental horizons, realizing the full potential within, and accepting the spiritual nature within all of us. The organization is world-wide; mind control is being taught in any language anywhere in the world, the group claims. It even awards a bachelor's and master's award in what it calls "psycho-orientology." Mind control graduates keep together the way graduates of other schools keep in touch.

Jose Silva began his research in 1944, eventually concentrating on brainwave control. "Our brain is functioning at the highest frequencies when we are the so-called conscious state," Mr. Silva explains in an outline of his method. "These frequencies, known as the beta frequencies, are typical of the five senses type of functioning; for example, your brain is now functioning at the beta frequency as you read. We know that the alpha brain frequencies are lower than the beta. We also know that theta and delta are brain frequencies lower than the alpha. The guiding concept in our research was to learn to use a lower brain frequency and apply its greater energy to make stronger impressions on the brain cells, since more information can be recalled when the information has been strongly impressed. Once psychological blockage is controlled, strong impressions of information on brain cells enhance retention and recall, factors contributory to an increased I.Q. factor."

The emphasis on brain versus mind in the Silva method must be disturbing to pure metaphysicians as it does seem to concentrate on the apparatus rather than the operator. Nevertheless, the results in some individuals are positive, while I am not aware of any harm being done by these classes. The Silva Mind Control establishment is extremely well organized, highly commercial in its approach, and reputable within the framework of its concept. Headquarters: Silva Mind Control, Post Office Box 1149, Laredo, Texas 78040. Telephone: 512-722-8622. **Satisfactory.**

Another worldwide organization, although on the other end of the spectrum of metaphysics, is the Eckankar movement, founded by the late Paul Twitchell. The movement is vaguely Eastern in its philosophy and terminology, believes in soul travel and soul mates, and advocates the law of love, even to extremes. "Never criticize, never find fault, never abuse, never even blame anyone either to his face or behind his back. Never hurt anyone's feelings, man or animal. Never permit harsh or unkind words to escape one's lips. Instead speak words of truth, of love and kindness." This is a quotation from Twitchell's letters to his wife Gail prior to their marriage. Twitchell is referred to as a sort of ascended prophet, and the current "incarnation" of the leading principle is a certain Sri Darwin Gross. The "Eck" movement, which was primarily a midwestern cult some ten years ago, has since spread all over the country and gone international as well. Groups have formed in many cities, including Los Angeles, San Francisco, New York, Chicago, and many smaller cities. Using East Indian terminology for their principles and the honorifics attached to their leaders, Eck also publishes books and a newsletter called the "Eck World News." It is difficult to compare this movement with any other philosophy, except that it doesn't seem to harm anyone, does not advocate violence or fanaticism, and seems to blend karmic concepts of the East with Western belief in self-improvement. Headquarters: Eckankar, Post Office box 5325, Las Vegas, Nevada 89102. **Satisfactory.**

"Back to the Godhead" is the battlecry of a movement that has been very much in evidence in our streets of late. Singing, dance-stepping young men and women, dressed in saffron robes, have been praising Krishna in monotonous, ill-modulated voices, creating a stir wherever they appear in small groups. The Hari Krishna movement, contrary to what some people think, is of comparatively recent origin and not one of the traditional Indian cults. In foresaking the material world for the praise of Krishna, the followers of this movement have seemingly gone to extremes, but the organization, despite its decidedly East Indian flavor, has attracted a number of Americans as well. There are branches now in major American cities. It publishes a magazine called *Back to the Godhead* and states its basic tenet as "Srimad-Bhagavatam the Sublime Science of the Supreme Personality of Godhead," whatever that means. For those who wonder, the movement's spiritual leaders supply an explanation. "It is all successful, all blissful, and all perfect. It is as bright as the sun. Thus, persons who have lost their vision due to the dense darkness of ignorance in the age of quarrel shall get light from it." To some the Hari Krishna movement is just one of the many religions of India, but it includes metaphysical concepts, the belief that "no one but Krishna can give protection and must therefore be surrendered to," so that its appeal lies well within the metaphysical sphere. Those wishing further information concerning this movement can write to: Bhaktivedanta Book Trust, 3764 Watseka Avenue, Los Angeles, California 90034. **No comment.**

The occult revival has been such that it has also attracted organizations that have little or nothing to do with the occult. But it seems like a good idea to cash in on the current interest in this field, and if possible, to reshape one's propaganda to fit in with this concept. A case in point is the well-known movement originally called Dianetics, and nowadays posing as a church under the name of Scientology. This worldwide organization is the brainchild of L. Ron Hubbard, one-time science fiction writer. Although the organization has been denounced by responsible psychic researchers, exposed by the likes of *Life* magazine, and even outlawed in some countries, such as Australia, it continues to thrive in this country. The basic concept of Scientology can lead to blackmail in that its operators obtain personal information from applicants under the guise of clearing up guilt feelings and other undesirable traits. Scientology now claims to have the answers to "your past life experiences," and that by helping you remember past lives, you will be able to appreciate this one more. I have personally met a number of Scientologists and found them extremely fanatic about their beliefs. Those in need of the services of a psychiatrist or a psychologist, but who turn to Scientology instead, are endangering their mental health. Others, not so in need, are nevertheless jeopardizing their emotional balance without deriving the slightest benefit from the association. **Not recommended.**

There are two more items of national connotation that

deserve listing here. One is the *Psychic Register International,* an ambitious undertaking by Bill and Elizabeth Finch of Phoenix, Arizona, which purports to be a *Who's Who* of the psychic world. The book does list hundreds upon hundreds of individuals connected with various phases of the occult, but it is totally uncritical and omits more than it includes. Written in a naive style, it is nevertheless useful to those seeking a pleasant neighborhood medium, or where the nearest convention of UFO enthusiasts is being held, or who is interested in the occult in your particular town. In this respect, it has undoubtedly brought many people together who would not otherwise know of each other's common interests. The *Psychic Register International* may be obtained from: Post Office Box 11288, Phoenix, Arizona 85017. **No comment.**

Finally, for those among students of the occult who wish to engage in some form of commercial enterprise, perhaps Sybil Leek's Aquarian Age Center might be just the thing. It consists of Sybil Leek's astro-prints for each sun sign, her notes (that is, stationery with the sun signs embossed on it), Sybil's scents, thirteen of the most popular incense fragrances, one for each sun sign, and her puzzles in full color. All this can be placed into the Astrobile, which is nothing more or less than an ingeniously designed display cabinet. The whole outfit can be obtained from: Post Office Box 3399, Albuquerque, New Mexico 87110. **Recommended.**

Arizona

There is a small but active occult community in Phoenix, and several bookshops catering to those interested in the subject. The Fountainhead, located in downtown Tucson, is another center for lectures and seminars. Those wishing to be kept informed of the program at the Fountainhead should write to: Post Office Box 50426, Tucson, Arizona 85703. Headquarters is located at 503 East Grant Road, Tucson. Telephone: 602-622-8974. **Satisfactory.**

The ARE in Phoenix maintains a medical center under the supervision of Dr. William McGarey. Patients are treated here in accordance with the philosophy of Edgar Cayce. The clinic is at Indian School Road, Phoenix, Arizona. **Recommended.**

Mr. and Mrs. William J. Finch, publishers of the *Psychic Register International*, leading activists in the occult field in Phoenix, may be reached at: 5519 North Thirty-fifth Drive, Phoenix, Arizona 85019. Telephone: 939-8693. **Satisfactory.**

Arkansas

Harold Sherman, the grand old man of ESP, respected medium and author on psychic subjects, has established the ESP Research Associates in Little Rock. This is a forum for lectures and discussions, with some group activity throughout the year, but with special seminars at certain times. The heart of it, however, is Mr. Sherman himself. ESP Research Associates publishes various pamphlets and books, although the majority of Mr. Sherman's work is published by various trade houses. Address: 1750 Tower Building, Little Rock, Arkansas 72201. **Recommended.**

California

It has been stated that California is the most fertile ground for anything having to do with the occult, and it has also been said that offbeat characters and weird people tend to congregate in this state. This is not quite true: the warm climate and the leisurely pace do attract people who like to meditate, people who do not like to work hard physically, and since so much of the life occurs outdoors, the area is conducive to discussions, forums, and religious activities in general. But the fact remains, that the two greatest concentrations of occult activities, both in terms of groups and individuals, can be found in New York City and in and around Los Angeles, California. Some of these activities are wholesome and extremely useful, some are merely harmless, and a few are downright phony and perhaps even dangerous. The following listing is by no means complete, as new individuals get into the field almost daily.

Triune Science of Being Awareness Center is a nonprofit organization offering a number of free programs throughout the year. Topics include Spiritualism, numerology, astrology, and psychic parties, if you will. "The ministry of the Triune Science of Being extends to encompass all areas of spiritual, mental and physical growth. Our main goal is to reach and help as many people as possible in whatever way we can. Part of this ministry involves our Silent Healing. Once each week our entire staff meets to focus its healing skills on individuals who need our help." Not everything at the center is free, of course, but admission to certain events is well within the range of average admissions to similar events elsewhere. The foundation has a schedule of classes, which are available to everyone. "Students experience the awakening of self through the esoteric teachings of astrology and numerology, the insights of psychology and group encounter, and the creative challenges of painting, sculpture, writing and more." Six week courses go for forty-five dollars, eight weeks for sixty dollars. Address: 3497 Cahuenga Boulevard, West Los Angeles, California 90068. Telephone: 213-851-3611. **Recommended.**

British-born Leagh Caverhill is the mainspring of the National Academy of Applied Awareness, Inc. Subjects covered by the classes taught by Miss Caverhill and several others include "man and his relationship to the universe," "mechanics of consciousness," "astral projection and astral travel," "reenergizing and self-protection techniques," and "Medinosis," which is explained as Miss Caverhill's new technique for reaching higher levels of consciousness at will. The founder of this academy was born in Burma of British parents and brought up in the East. She is described as a psychic and healer, much of her wisdom acquired while a student in the Himalayas. The Academy has been heavily publicized in various media and seems bent on attracting public attention. Address: 6255 Sunset Boulevard, Hollywood, California 90028. Telephone: 213-461-3831. **Satisfactory.**

Academies seem to be in style this season. The Academy of Atlantis, billed as a School of Occult Sciences, is presently under the leadership of Larry Fanning and an extraordinary psychic and trance medium, Donna Marshall. Their curriculum includes a full description of life in old Atlantis and the story of Jesus, which seems to connect with the Edgar Cayce material. Several other courses are also taught, including psychic and spiritual awareness, mystic Bible interpretation, and Hatha Yoga. Classes are $2.50 a class, and courses of four weeks run to twenty-four dollars. Address: 12001 Wilshire Boulevard, Los Angeles, California. Telephone: 213-826-5615. **Satisfactory.**

If you've never heard of the Arica Institute, Inc., you are not alone. I hadn't either until I came across their material and activities. But apparently they have teaching houses in New York City, Honolulu, Los Angeles, San Diego, and several other towns. "Everything you need is already within you" goes the catch-phrase used in their advertisements. "Arica is a totally new experience which combines the wisdom of the past with modern scientific knowledge to solve the problems of the present. Arica is a system of scientific mysticism. The goal of the individual is unity, unity within each person, between persons, and within the society as a whole." In the Los Angeles area, the Arica Institute is located at: 9916 Santa Monica Boulevard, Beverly Hills, California. Telephone: 213-277-7641. **Satisfactory.**

The Self Realization Fellowship is a metaphysical concept of living, nonsectarian but very much religiously oriented. Some pretty solid citizens belong to this philosophy, and the fellowship publishes pamphlets that explain their theories of self-development. In Los Angeles the address is: 3880 San Raphael Avenue, Los Angeles, California 90065. **Recommended.**

The Philosphical Research Society was at one time one of the "in" groups among occult elitists. The society published the works of Manly P. Hall and sponsored lectures on various aspects of metaphysical philosophy. Those wishing to learn of its present programs may write to: 3910 Los Feliz Boulevard, Los Angeles, California 90027. **Recommended.**

J. Wilfrid Hahn, Ph.D., is the director of the Mind Science Foundation. Dr. Hahn pursues primarily a research program, and the foundation is not looking for publicity or public acclaim. It does, however, have a small program for students. Address: 6001 West Ninety-eighth Street, Los Angeles, California 90045. **Recommended.**

The following are smaller groups, sometimes only one or two teachers working out of a rented hall or center, with group sessions and classes as well as individual, private consultations. They have not been rated as to their relative importance or reliability.

Marina Mind Science Center, Jim Lytle, teacher, Venice, California, telephone 213-399-7534. "Exploring many paths on the journey toward ultimate realization and freedom." The Personal Creative Freedoms Foundations, 1700 Westwood Boulevard, Westwood, California 90024, telephone 916-474-1565, offers a psychic ability test and classes in various aspects of the occult. The Center For Spiritual Studies, 415 South Topanga Canyon Boulevard, Topanga, California 90290, telephone 455-1046, hold daily classes in Yoga, chanting and meditation, and deals mainly in Eastern philosophical concepts of metaphysics. Similarly, the Sivananad Yoga Vedanta Center, a nonprofit association at 115 North Larchmont

Boulevard, Los Angeles, California 90004, telephone 213-464-1276, offers students the complete study of the various forms of Yoga, of which there are five—Hatha Yoga, Bahkti Yoga, Karma Yoga, Ganana Yoga, and Raja Yoga. Annual registration at the center is five dollars, Yoga classes are two dollars each. This is hardly a commercial enterprise. In the same general vein, the Guru Ram Das Ashram at 1620 Preuss Road, Los Angeles, California 90035, telephone 213-273-9422, offers various forms of Yoga training. The Astara Foundation, labelled nonprofit, but heavily advertised in various occult magazines, is essentially the brainchild of Robert and Earlyne Chaney, spiritual mediums. They promise the unraveling of the mystery of man, and describe Astara as a "worldwide non-profit organization created for one purpose —to help you. If you seek a richer fuller life with meaning and purpose, write now for the free booklet, 'Finding Your Peace in the Golden Age.' " Astara headquarters is at 261 South Mariposa Avenue, Los Angeles, California 90004.

The ESP Laboratory, headed by Al G. Manning, promises to help people with ESP training, white witchcraft and other sundries. Mr. Manning also advertises in *Fate* magazine and elsewhere, and there is an attractive sign atop his little building so that those who happen to be passing by will become aware of his activities. The "laboratory" is located at: 7559 Santa Monica Boulevard, Los Angeles, California 90046. **No comment.**

The Institute of Mentalphysics not only offers seminars in the teaching of this newly named subject but also advertises its location as an ideal vacation spot. "For two weeks in a veritable paradise you will recharge your body and open your mind to the inspirational practices of Mentalphysics (Pranayama, meditation, chanting and transmutation)." Address: Post Office Box 640, Yucca Valley, California 92284. **No comment.**

Unarius, describing itself as Science of Life, is being administered by its founders, Dr. Ernest L. and Ruth E. Norman. Its stationery states that "inter-planetary communications are now a fact," misspelling the word *interplanetary* in the process, and pointing to the fact that members of the group, the Unarians, have been receiving mental transmissions through the intergalatic system since August 2, 1973. Not satisfied with proclaiming this marvelous news of interplay between the people from Venus, Eros, Hermes, Orion, and other planets, Unarius publishes a veritable library of pamphlets describing these metaphysical messages in great detail. There is also a tape library, keeping up with the latest in technology, promising the buyer, "conclave of the Light Beings book or tapes will take you on a psychic trip to the super celestial city atop the heavenly crystal plateau, upon which rests the great golden conical Temple of Light, wherein is being held a tumultous celebration, commemoration of the New Golden Age just arrived. You will be shown all about this heavenly structure, the conical temple of golden crystal, and all existent therein! You will witness the entire ceremony of the archangels and the spiritual marriage of two god forces." Despite the many grammatical errors in its literature, the pamphlets published by this organization are professionally done and interestingly written. "To attempt to describe Unarius would be like trying to place all the visible and invisible universes into the proverbial goldfish bowl, for Unarius does encompass all known and unknown elements and factors of life and the creative principles which make all things possible," the introduction to Unarius states without undue modesty. This "school" maintains a mail order course, and does not encourage students to call at its headquarters. Unarius is located at: Post Office Box 1042, El Cajon, California 92022. **No comment.**

The Whittier Psychic Society is not a scientific research

body but a small group of serious students of the occult and of parapsychology grouped around a local hypnotist with an interest in parapsychology. The group meets on the first and third Saturday of each month and covers discussions and lectures on every aspect of the occult. Those in the area who may be interested in its activities should write to: Post Office Box 4103, Whittier, California 90607. Telephone: 213-693-2321. **Satisfactory.**

San Jose, California, is the headquarters of the Rosicrucian Lodge also known as AMORC. This is based on the old Order of the Rosy Cross, as it existed in seventeenth-century Germany. During the last century, it was revived and brought to America by a California businessman and has since flourished nationally. Rosicrucianism is a gentle philosophy of life, built upon the concept of reincarnation and a life filled with love for one another. Enlightenment comes because of the life one leads, and not because of special rituals or occult practices. More than anything, Rosicrucians have a way of life that differs markedly from the ordinary materialistic concept in the approach to problems, to human relationships, to food and diet, and in religious worship. The Rosicrucians publish a long line of pamphlets and books explaining their philosophy in greater detail. Headquarters of AMORC are at San Jose, California 95114. **Recommended.**

Florida

The Lotus Metaphysical Center, Inc. of Miami is built around the well-known personality of Reverend Noel Street. Mr. Street is a British-born psychic healer and medium who travels a great deal and demonstrates his psychic skills worldwide. He is also the author of a number of books and markets a home study series dealing with such subjects as the Akashic Records, reincarnation and the law of consequence, the human aura, and, probably unique in this field, psychic healing with the Maori Indians in New Zealand. (This must also be the first time the Maoris were referred to as Indians.) Those wishing to obtain Mr. Street's mail order study courses should write to the Center at Miami, Florida, and those wishing private consultations will probably be able to catch up with him somewhere along the line, as he tours a great deal. Address: 128 N.E. Eighty-second Terrace, Miami, Florida 33138. **Satisfactory.**

Georgia

The Atlanta Institute of Metaphysics is probably the best and most reputable organization in the greater Atlanta area. It was founded a few years ago by Mr. and Mrs. Peter Calhoun, when Peter Calhoun became disillusioned with the orthodox ministry he then held. Consequently he turned to a spiritual path and has since become one of the better known mediums in the Atlanta area. In addition to his own private work, he operates a center where a regular schedule of lectures and teaching sessions is being maintained. The center also sells pamphlets and books and acts as a kind of clearing-house for psychic activities in the area. Address: 1625 Monroe Drive, Atlanta, Georgia 30324. Telephone: 404-875-0273. **Definitely recommended.**

Belle Gorman has for the past few years tried to maintain a small study group called the Parapsychology Forum of Decatur. The group organizes occasional lectures and discussion groups at the DeKalb YMCA Center. Mrs. Gorman may be reached by writing to her at: 1713 Atherton Circle, Decatur, Georgia 30032. **Recommended.**

Louisiana

There are perhaps two dozen groups in the greater New Orleans area that should be of interest to those involved with the occult sciences. A good way to acquaint oneself with the details of these groups is through a publication called *Esoteric Coordinating News*, published by Donna M. France: 1012 Pasadena Street, Metairie, Louisiana 70001. Telephone: 504-831-1344.

There are three organizations claiming the classification as psychic research institutes in New Orleans. First, the Parapsychology Research Foundation of the South, founded and run by the hypnotist Clem Zane and his daughter Dawn. Address: 6131 Hurst Street, New Orleans, Louisiana 70118. **No comment.**

The Psychic Research Society of greater New Orleans is headed by Ernest Haldeman, a performing magician. Mr. Haldeman's group arranges seminars and discussion groups and has a membership numbering several hundreds. Address: Box 50206, New Orleans, Louisiana 70150. **Satisfactory.**

The Institute for the Realization of Personal Potential is headed by Alex Keller. This group prefers metaphysical exercises, including much Eastern philosophy, to intellectual discussions on a parapsychological level. Those wishing information about the lectures and classes of this group can write to: 916 Howard Avenue, New Orleans, Louisiana 70113. Telephone: 504-581-1656. **No comment.**

Minnesota

Bearded Carl Weschke heads an empire of occult activities built mainly on the foundation of his Llewellyn Publications, publisher of books and magazines on various occult topics. Mr. Weschke also likes sponsoring witchcraft conventions, and through one of his magazines, he organizes Gnostic festivals every year. Affiliated with Mr. Weschke's organization is the Gnostic Study Center in Minneapolis, Minnesota, where students can learn various aspects of the occult from astrology to witchcraft, from ESP to meditation. Many of the not-so-famous professionals in the occult field are regular performers at Mr. Weschke's conventions and study courses, and though he does not run the largest occult publishing house in America, as he is quoted in a recent newspaper story, he does run a pretty successful operation. Address: Gnostic Study Center, 1414 Lorell Avenue, Minneapolis, Minnesota 55400. **No comment.**

New York

The New York Spiritualist Center, Inc. of New York City is under the direction of William and Renee Linn, two dedicated Spiritualists who are also healers. The center sponsors regular Sunday meetings and gives classes in spiritual development during the week. This is a conventional Spiritualist group, organized along religious lines, thoroughly honest in its approach and somewhat pastoral in the content of its messages. Like much of American Spiritualism, it is part church and part psychic communication center. British Spiritualists tend to shy away from the church affiliation and leave the sermons and biblical classes to the orthodox estalishment. The Linns are also psychic healers and conduct regular healing services at their center. Those wishing to obtain schedules should write to: Rev. William Linn, New York Spiritualist Center, Inc., 225 East Seventy-fourth Street, New York, New York 10021. **Recommended.**

Gopi Krishna is an author living in Switzerland who has written a number of books on mystical experience and the evolutionary process. Now in his seventies, Krishna is considered an Indian philosopher who has apparently rediscovered the importance of Kundalini, the creative life force in man, upon the attainment of a state of genius. What makes Mr. Gopi Krishna different from other Indian philosophers is his claim that this life force can and should be investigated by orthodox scientists, using orthodox scientific methods. The

Kundalini Research Foundation, the brainchild of an advertising executive named Gene Kieffer, is trying very hard to interest the trade press and the scientific establishment in Mr. Krishna's discoveries. Those interested in this subject may obtain pamphlets and further information on the Krishna approach from: Kundalini Research Foundation, 10 East Thirty-ninth Street, New York, New York 10016. Telephone: 212-889-3241. **No comment.**

Spectrum is a forum for lectures on various aspects of the occult under the direction of Rita Livingston. Regular lectures and forums are held periodocially and those wishing to take part in them should contact Spectrum at the following address: 49 East Ninety-first Street, New York, New York 10028. Telephone: 212-289-7005. **No comment.**

Serenity Socials is a newly formed group meeting every Saturday night at the East-West Nataraj Restaurant for "short talks, music, poetry, conversation, subjects: inner vibrational harmony, nutrition, yoga, occult, acquarian age, ecology, art of living, cosmic consciousness. Enjoy meeting people of similar interest." This group is under the guidance of Henry Casper, philosopher and student of the occult. Restaurant address: 15 East Thirty-first Street, New York, New York 10016. **Recommended.**

The Sixth Sense is not a forum, not a bogus television program, but a mail-order supply house for everything needed by the occultist, from zodiac amulets to robes, from love oil to lamp oil, from mystical candies to love potions, guaranteed to "create a greater harmony in your love life." This "line" is the brainchild of Saul P. Larner, sometime astrologer, and the address is simply: Applied Awareness Associates, New York, New York 10021. **No comment.**

The Wainwright Center in Rye, New York, is a forum that sponsors discussions and lecturers in various branches of the occult from time to time. Generally held on weekends, these informal classes are limited to something like forty participants. Those wishing to obtain information on the current program should write: Wainwright Center, 260 Stuyvesant Avenue, Rye, New York 10580. **Satisfactory.**

Amerisyche is the peculiar name given to a small organization dedicated to the exploration of every phase of the occult, basically on an extremely esoteric and intellectual level. Amerisyche stands for The American Society for Astropsychical Research and publishes a newsletter, much of it the work of its leading genius, who uses the name of Merlin Solomon. By profession an illustrator and writer, Mr. Solomon explores many aspects of the occult rarely mentioned in more mundane publications. Those interested in this group and the newsletter should write: Amerisyche, 141 Arsenal Street, Watertown, New York 13601. **Recommended.**

Pennsylvania

A casual discussion and lecture program has been organized in the greater Pittsburgh area by Mrs. Stephanie Grove. This includes all aspects of parapsychology and the occult, but does not as yet have a regular lecture series or classes. Those in the area who are interested in the field should correspond with Mrs. Grove at: 605 Grandview Avenue, East Pittsburgh, Pennsylvania 15112. **Recommended.**

The Chapel of The Living Presence is the rather high sounding name for a metaphysical group led by Mildred Gourlay, meeting for Sunday services and Tuesday evening sessions. The good reverend, when in trance, brings messages not only from some exalted masters but also from the late President Lincoln. Somehow I cannot quite imagine President Lincoln saying, "Greetings everyone." On the other hand, the reverend also brings through Herbert Hoover who is quoted as admonishing the country to stop "wrangling with each other."

The late president then adds, "let us have a stop to this. Put the dove of peace above the dome of the Capitol. Place it there, and there it shall be." It just doesn't sound like ole Herbert Hoover at all. Those who still wish to inform themselves concerning this center, may write: Chapel of The Living Presence, 528 Lewis Road, Limerick, Pennsylvania 19468. **No comment.**

For many years the Spiritualist movement has maintained a fine record of honesty and service. Not all mediums working as Spiritualist reverends were gifted, some were merely talented as pastoral advisors—and a few were downright frauds. This is not surprising, because mediumship is a human profession, and there are honest and dishonest individuals in every line of work. A few years ago, some of the fraudulent mediums practicing their art at various Spiritualist camps around the country were properly exposed as frauds, especially those pretending to present materialization phenomena of departed ones. Despite the considerable amount of publicity given to these exposures both in the mundane and the Spiritualist press, the same individuals returned to the camps year after year, practicing their deceit, because there are still people who desire to be deceived, simply because they need the crutch of belief. One of the camps mentioned as having its share of fraudulent mediums is Silver Belle at Ephrata, Pennsylvania. Like other Spiritualist camps in America, it is well organized, and during the summer a considerable number of resident mediums cater to every taste from clairvoyance to materialization seances. When I requested permission to investigate the materialization mediums at the camp, I received a list of those working in this field together with the admonition that neither cameras nor tape recorders were allowed at the camp. Without testing equipment, a visit would be of little use, so I declined. Those sitting for materialization at camp Silver Belle include F. Reed Brown, Roy Burkholder,

William J. Donnelly, James W. Gordon, and Warren M. Smith. Of this group, I am only familiar with the work of Donnelly and Smith. For the record, camp Silver Belle is at Ephrata, Pennsylvania, has been in existence since 1932, and is situated on Route 322, East Main Street, two blocks east of the Ephrata business center. Telephone 717-733-2503. **Not recommended.**

Texas

Things in the Lone Star State are always a little bigger and a little louder than elsewhere. So it doesn't come as a special surprise that the Church of Humanity, led by the Reverend Russ Michael is also the sponsor of the annual Dallas Psychic Arts Fair at the convention center in Dallas. This includes lectures, resident psychics, booths where books and psychic equipment may be purchased, and such fascinating lecturers as Noel Street and his wife Coleen; yoga instructor Bevey Jaegers of St. Louis, a vociferous and self-assured medium; prophetess Bernadine Villanueva of Tampa, Florida; and last, but certainly not least, Komar the famous fakir, whose alter ego manufactures some excellent cheese in Wooster, Ohio, when he is not busy fakiring. Reverend Russ Michael is a capable psychic himself, and those wishing to contact this center should write: Church of Humanity, 4503 Glenwick Lane, Dallas, Texas 75205. **Satisfactory.**

Houston also has a number of active groups in the field. There is the Esoteric Philosophy Center at 523 Lovett Boulevard, Houston, Texas (telephone: 713-524-7758), which sponsors lectures and forum discussions. If altered consciousness training is your need, contact the Creative Study Center at 4500 Mountrose, Houston (telephone: 713-667-7332). Beyond mind dynamics and mental control are taught by Robert B. Wright at the Optimum Center, and you can get information on these courses at 713-667-1530. There is even a publication called *The Cosmic Echo,* listing all of these activities regularly. It may be obtained at: 4500 Mountrose, Houston, Texas 77006. **Satisfactory.**

Canada

If you happen to live in Canada and have need for some extremely obtuse esoteric messages, perhaps Light Affiliates of British Columbia might be your cup of tea. This group publishes a newsletter in which the sayings of a certain Esu are printed verbatim, and there are also messages from a certain Michael, concerning the world, the comet Kohoutek, the sun spots, and all sorts of useful information. As with so many of these religious-metaphysical messages, the emphasis is on the need for man's evolution through love, honesty, and freedom. It doesn't tell you how to do it, however. It merely indicates what ought to be done. Those interested in Light Affiliates and its newsletter may write: Box 431, South Burnaby, British Columbia, Canada. **No comment.**

Undoubtedly, there are many more groups, some good, some bad, some mediocre. As I learn of them and their activities, and have the chance to look into them personally, I will attempt to list them in future editions of the book.

4

Individual Practitioners
Mediums, Readers, Psychics, Astrologers, and Other Purveyors of Occult Information

The number of letters I get every week requesting the name of a reputable medium or other occult practitioner in a particular city or area is staggering. In fact, it is the one question most readers ask of me. There seems to be such a need to consult with an occultist that one cannot simply explain it as a weakness of character in the person requesting such services, or as curiosity, or as the need to get in touch with a dead relative. The ground swell of psychic interest is so strong, permeating so many layers of our present society, that the overriding reason for wanting to meet with a professional psychic is one of intellectual seeking rather than of personal gain. True, perhaps as many as one-third of those writing to me for the name of a competent medium have a personal reason for doing so. Perhaps someone dear has died, and the writer would like to know why the dear one hasn't been in touch with them; or perhaps the writer's life or career has not gone well, and he needs some advice, if possible from the "other side" of life. But many more people find the possibility of ESP development, the probability that some individuals can foretell the future and may do so for them, the entire frontier of the mind phenomena as such, the impelling force for seeking out psychically gifted individuals. Under the circumstances, I would like to lay down some ground rules applying to the listings that follow.

To begin with, there are literally thousands of qualified practitioners of the various branches of the occult sciences that do not appear in this book simply because I haven't met them. I do not list here anyone I do not personally know, or of whose work I haven't been informed by reliable observers. Also, since I live in New York City and travel primarily to the major population centers, most of those listed in these pages will be in the large cities. But there are some excellent psychics and astrologers in the hinterlands as well, whose names will eventually appear in the pages of future editions of this book. My criteria for the acceptance of an occult practitioner in these pages is based on performance and reputation: performance in the sense that a reading or several readings given by this person has been reasonably evidential and cannot be explained on the grounds of foreknowledge, guesswork, or generalities; reputation in that the person involved does not charge excessively for his or her services, does not make claims that are unsupported by the evidence on hand, and has not been involved in any fraudulent practices. In no way do I guarantee the people of whom I write here, nor do I represent them in any way. All contacts must be made between the seeker and the practitioner directly. I advise my readers always to inquire as to the fee involved *prior* to seeking an appointment with a specific individual. I realize that it is difficult for many to travel into cities where such practitioners work, but there really isn't any substitute for personal sittings. Readings by mail, which are given by some professionals in this field, are rarely evidential, and I advise my readers not to ask for them. It is unfair to the psychic or other practitioner involved, because the vibration cannot be as strong as when the sitter is in front of them. It is also unwise on the part of the writer, since he is trying to get something the easy way, and thus exposes himself to failure, if not fraud. Readings on the telephone have sometimes succeeded; however, this is primarily true of cases in which a previous personal contact has already taken place and the telephone contact is merely a follow up. The only exception to the rule of "no readings by mail" are astrologers who cast horoscopes not through their psychic abilities but by mathematical computation. In the case of astrologers, only the exact data of birth are required; a personal meeting is in fact generally frowned upon by leading astrologers, at least until after the chart has been drawn.

In a later chapter, I will go deeper into the methods used in psychic readings and the behavior most conducive for success as far as the sitter is concerned. The listings are geographical, and alphabetical by states.

Alaska

There is an active Wicca circle of white witchcraft in Anchorage, who also perform psychic healing work. The group is small, consists of local people active in various professions, and welcomes strangers if they come motivated by genuine interest in the Wicca religion, or seek help in this particular way. The group may be contacted by writing: Mrs. Mia Lamoureaux, Box 8151, Anchorage, Alaska 99504. **Recommended.**

Arizona

Mr. and Mrs. Robert Evanston, a young couple dedicated to a middle-of-the-road program of lectures, group discussions, and meetings, are also the Phoenix representatives of Spiritual Frontiers Fellowship. Both are psychic and can arrange for private sittings. Address: 1018 West Mitchell Drive, Phoenix, Arizona 85213. Telephone: 602-263-5394. **Recommended.**

The Universal Truth Foundation, headed by Norma J. Graham, is a small group of people interested in the occult who meet for discussions and seminars. Miss Graham may be reached at: 4340 North Seventh Avenue, Phoenix, Arizona 85203. **Satisfactory.**

California

The number of occult practitioners in California is very large, but the number of truly first-rate mediums is disappointingly small. This is especially true in the case of trance mediums. On the other hand, California seems to be strong on good astrologers, as well as some of the more unusual forms of divination, such as numerology and its various offshoots.

George Daisley, British-born Spiritualist minister, came to public attention because of the work he did with the late Bishop James Pike. Reverend Daisley was able to give the bishop a tremendously evidential reading, whereby the bishop's late son manifested in trance to the full satisfaction of Bishop Pike and his associates. This was the more astounding as Mr. Daisley had no idea what the connection was; he did not recognize the bishop, and the alleged personality of the bishop's son, Jim Jr., referred to a conversation that had been started some time prior in England through another medium, Ena Twigg, something of which Mr. Daisley would have been totally unaware. Since that time, many have beaten a path to Mr. Daisley's door, to the point of his not being as easy to see as he once was. This is the more regrettable as he is one of the best mediums around. His personal life, his pastoral approach to the work he does, the quiet, British stance he takes, are the very image of Spiritualism in general. And the fact that he is extremely evidential in his readings makes him that much more valuable to the field in which he works. Those wishing a sitting with George Daisley should write to him first, and under no circumstances drop in or in any way expect an immediate sitting. Address: 629 San Isidro Road, Santa Barbara, California 93108. Telephone: 805-687-1873. **Recommended.**

The "Great Lady" among Los Angeles mediums is octogenarian Lotte von Strahl, a Dutch-born psychic who was once married to a diplomat and who turned to psychic work as a means of support some years ago when she came to the United States and found there was no other work to be had for someone of her background. She has worked with medical doctors as a healer, and she has worked with the researchers at U.C.L.A. in haunted houses. However, her main claim to fame these days are the many movie stars who come to consult her. Among those for whom she predicted fame was Goldie Hawn, at a time when the blond actress was just beginning to be noticed. Miss von Strahl lives in a comfortable house in Westwood, furnished in exquisite European taste, with the framed photographs of some of her famous clients scattered around the room. She resents being compared to a fortune-teller, which she isn't, and considers her work that of a consultant, since she mingles a great deal of psychology in with her psychic readings. I found her reading of me quite eloquent. Among many other things, she predicted I would write a screenplay at a time when no such possibility seemed on the horizon. As I write these lines, I am weighing the offer of two screenplays, with a third a distinct possibility. Miss von Strahl has very definite opinions concerning the hereafter, and concerning the work she does, which are not necessarily identical with the opinions of those with whom she works. She is an aristocratic lady and sees people by appointment only. Those wishing to have a consultation with her should write: 437 Gayly Avenue, Westwood, California 96137. **Recommended.**

Probably the most illusive of all California mediums is Bill Corrado. He received a great deal of publicity by being mentioned in the books of Jess Stearn, and subsequently because of his association with a well-known industrial company, which took him away a great deal. I was finally able to corner Mr. Corrado at the home of astrologer Betty Collins, and on December 15, 1973, I sat face to face with the slight, dark-haired young man of whom I'd heard so much.

"I was born in Cleveland, Ohio," Mr. Corrado explained. "Both my mother and my grandmother were psychic, although not professionals. I grew up in that environment, and when I was six years old, my own talent came out. For five days in succession, I had a vision of an auto accident in which my father figured, and I told my mother but was advised not to think about it. On the sixth day, my father was killed in an auto accident. From then on, these visions came more frequently, but I did not use my gift professionally until I came to California in 1962. I studied for the priesthood for two-and-a-half years in a Benedictine seminary, and then I left and worked as an auditor for the real estate tax department. And at one time I was also a probation officer for the police in Cleveland. When I came out to California, I first became a medic, taking care of people on welfare in their own homes, but I had some surgery which paralyzed me for a while so I could no longer work. It was then that I started to give professional readings, first to friends of mine, and they in turn started sending people to me. And before I knew what had happened, that was all I was doing, giving professional readings."

I asked Mr. Corrado whether he was advising some important business people, as I had been told.

"Yes," he nodded, "I specialize in advising corporations concerning different investments and marketing systems. I also advise on who is to be promoted, who is to be fired, who is to be hired."

"Do you get impressions about events in the future visually, or do you hear them, or do you get them from spirits?"

"Sometimes I've heard the sound of a voice, but most of my impressions are visual. I feel it is part of my mind which is more developed, so to speak, and able to tune in to what I call the universal mind."

"Have you ever seen a spirit communicator?"

"No."

I asked Bill Corrado to give me some specific examples of his being able to call the shots in people's lives. He explained that in addition to his financial wizardry he has done much work in the field of medical diagnosis and works with various medical doctors.

"I don't heal anyone, but I've been able to tell people what their illnesses are, where they are, and then I send them to a medical doctor to have it verified and let them be treated. I've been able to prescribe certain types of vitamins which have proved to be successful and have cured people. As you know, I also advise a lot of companies, some of them drilling for oil, others I help organize marketing plans in the cosmetic and vitamin field. I advise a lot of people in the entertainment world, when they come to me with a script and ask me whether or not the film will be good or not and whether they should do it. So far, I've not made many mistakes. For instance, for the last two years I've helped a man at the head of a large cosmetic company called Hollywood Magic, William Penn Patrick, who has recently passed away. I've also worked with politicians and assisted the police and sherrif's department of Los Angeles in different cases. For instance, when the Tate murder occurred, the police came to me and asked if I had any feelings about it. That was in May of that year, and I told them I saw three people involved in the murder, and they would all be apprehended in October of the same year. It turned out that they were apprehended in October. I've also been able to help people with emotional problems, for I consider a psychic to be part psychiatrist, part medical doctor, part teacher, and part businessman. Psychiatrists come to me with their files of people they handle, when they are unable to succeed with them, and many times I was able to pinpoint the real problem for them. This was especially true with people who have tried to commit suicide more than once."

"Do you compare your work in diagnosis to the work of the late Edgar Cayce?"

"Yes, I do."

Bill Corrado is hard to reach because he travels a great deal. But when he is in Los Angeles, he gives three to four readings a day, four days a week. Corrado is thirty-five years old, and has numerous calls from people who want to see him, even from abroad. "Most know about me from word of mouth," he explained. "I've been on many television shows, and some people have written about me."

"What percentage of your predictions have actually come true as made?" I asked.

"My average of accuracy has been about eighty-three percent," Bill Corrado replied without batting an eye. He insists that his clients tape-record the readings and that they report to him the accuracy of his predictions so that he may keep up with the results of his work.

Since Corrado hadn't met me before, I asked him whether on first contact he received any impressions about me. Corrado proceeded to give an extremely accurate reading of my personal life at the time, of which he could not have had any knowledge; he also predicted that I would be doing writing outside the psychic field, and that is coming true as I write these lines.

He stressed the need for some sort of test for psychics, to differentiate between reputable practitioners and those masquerading as mediums when in fact they have no talent or training. He himself has opened a school. "I will teach people how to use the amount of psychic ability they have so that they will be able to tune in to certain events in other people's lives as well as their own, teach them how to handle their emotional problems in a way where they can see a cure. It will be a five-day course and will be held here in Los Angeles. Later I expect to open schools in other cities around the United States, Canada, and even Europe." Mr. Corrado sees Los Angeles as a spiritual center, he's not worried about earthquakes, but has doubts about the safety of the San Francisco area.

Those interested in Mr. Corrado's Mind School may write to him about the program. Mr. Corrado's fee for general readings is fifty dollars, but he stresses that he has done readings for as little as ten or twenty dollars and even nothing at all if someone is "in very bad condition and doesn't have the money but needs the reading" because he feels he can make up such loss of income from the fees paid him by commercial companies and corporations. Those who hope to get a private reading from the renowned psychic may apply by mail to: Bill Corrado, 23243 Burbank Boulevard, Beverly Hills, California. **Recommended.**

The Reverend Estella Barnes, who calls herself an English Medium-Healer, works in the Los Angeles area as a Spiritualist medium and performs religious services as well at the First Church of Psychic Science, Inc., and the College for Mediums on Sundays and Wednesdays. She even gives instructions by mail concerning "unfoldment in mediumship."

I first met Mrs. Barnes in May, 1969, in Hollywood. She has been psychic since age four, but in the United States she has specialized in murder cases, hauntings, search for lost individuals, and spirit photography, in addition to her teaching activities. She says that "my timely warning saved the lives of two of our presidents, Truman and Eisenhower, by my contacting the Washington, D.C., authorities months ahead of the times the assassinations were to be carried out. I have also helped Scotland Yard in murder cases."

Mrs. Barnes, who knew nothing about me except what had been published in my books up to 1969, then proceeded to give me a reading. It was mostly personal, and there were several interesting items in it. For example, she saw me connected with the royal family of Russia. She claimed that the late czar was speaking to her in spirit and asking me to help Grand

Duchess Anastasia. It so happens that I went to see the alleged grand duchess in 1973 but was prevented from speaking to her directly by her husband. Mrs. Barnes insisted that the lady in Virginia is the true daughter of the czar, contrary to some opinions held by others. She then wondered whether I was linked up with the royal family of Russia. She could not know, of course, that my wife Catherine is a direct descendant of Catherine the Great of Russia.

Mrs. Estella Barnes can be reached at: 5018 South Western Avenue, Los Angeles, California 90062. Telephone: 213-AX3-2668. **Satisfactory.**

Also in the Los Angeles area, though somewhat remote from the center, is the location of the Reverend Allene Albano. Reverend Albano runs a shop called The Prophet, which sells oils, herbs, incense, candles, books *and* ancient secrets. I do not know what the ancient secrets are, but Reverend Albano gives sittings by appointment. She is located at: 16708 Bellflower Boulevard, Bellflower, California 90706. Telephone: 213-925-5214. **Satisfactory.**

The Reverend De A'Morelli has written a number of pamphlets on numerology and psychic powers, the most notable of which is *The Occult Encyclopedia.* A somewhat nervous, shy young man, Mr. De A'Morelli calls his personal organization The Cosmic Brotherhood, "an occult lodge dedicated to psychical research." He may be reached for private readings at: 6227 Craner Street, North Hollywood, California 91606. **Satisfactory.**

Ernesto Montgomery is a seer who likes to make large-scale predictions, especially in the headlines. This personable black man has compared himself to the late Edgar Cayce in his publicity releases, which may be a trifle out of line. But he does have the reputation of a good psychic reader, and those wishing to try him may reach him at 213-731-9207 in Los Angeles, California. **Satisfactory.**

Michael Hughes, Ph.D, makes his money in real estate but doubles as a professional psychic reader. He is very popular with the ladies, gives a polished and personable impression, and though his readings are largely metaphysical, has frequently hit on very evidential material as well. He may be reached at: 1632 North Gardner Street, Hollywood, California 90046. Telephone: 213-874-0136. **Satisfactory.**

Though he makes no predictions for the future, the Reverend Richard Zenor of the Agasha Temple of Wisdom, Inc., of Hollywood is well known beyond the local area. His temple compares favorably with any established church, his services are as inspiring as any liberal Christian service is, his following is large, and his position one of great respectability. What makes him somewhat different from any religious minister, even of a nondenominational variety, is the fact that at heart Mr. Zenor is a trance medium. Agasha is the name of the mysterious Eastern master who allegedly speaks through him, although there are several other guides who dispense wisdom and information to those seeking a private audience with the Reverend. I met Richard Zenor for the first time in 1968, and even addressed his congregation on one occasion. They seemed to be mainly middle-class people, but include some youngsters as well as some decidedly Spiritualist believers. In addition to the conventional pastoral talk, Zenor gives psychic readings from the pulpit, and in this respect does not differ greatly from other Spiritualist ministers. However, much of his work is done in deep trance. During several private sittings I had with him, I was impressed with the sincerity of his work, and with the metaphysical content of the messages received from his spirit guides. I did not receive anything evidential in the strictest sense of the term, but Zenor had not promised me any such material. For those who seek a religion based on spiritual experience, the Agasha Temple of Wisdom, Inc., is not a bad place to go to be spiritually elevated and perhaps to make friends with similarly minded people. The temple is prospering, the following large, allowing Mr. and Mrs. Zenor to live on a country estate in nearby Tarzana. Those seeking admission to the temple should contact Richard Zenor at: Agasha Temple of Wisdom, Inc., 460 North Western Avenue, Los Angeles, California 90004. Telephone: 213-HO4-6252. **Recommended.**

Reminiscent of some of the practitioners of the occult found in the old French Quarter of New Orleans is the Reverend Esther Washington, who runs a religious candle shop, under the motto of "for thou wilt light my candle: the Lord my God will enlighten my darkness." She assures her potential followers that "millions are fixed or hexed. Are you demon possessed? Open new dimensions of your mind and abolish crossed condition. There is no pity for those knowing they are in hard luck and need help. One visit will convince you." Those wishing to be enlightened by Lady Esther may find her at: 1046 West Highland Avenue, San Bernardino, California 92405. Telephone: 714-882-1113. **No comment.**

Jack Horner, at least this Jack Horner, did not sit in the corner but runs something called the "Personal Creative Freedoms Foundation," which specializes in "Incarnation Awareness Assessment." Mr. Horner assures one and all that this is not fortune-telling, nor is it hypnotism, but the first time something like this has been made available to the general public.

"The primary purposes of Eductivism and the Personal Creative Freedoms Foundation are not to prove or research past lives, but anything that can assist you to expand your available self understanding is of value and the Incarnation Awareness Assessment certainly does that."

Although it sounds somewhat like the infamous life readings frequently dispensed at fees from fifty to one hundred dollars to those gullible enough to ask for them, Mr. Horner seems to specialize more in the assessment of present potential rather than past glories. **No comment.**

Leo Wagner has long sought to prove to me how good a psychic he really is. Eventually I met him in Hollywood and asked him to describe himself. "I am an inspirator and intuitionist," Mr. Wagner, a middle-aged, slightly pudgy gentleman explained. "In other words, I speak as I am guided to speak."

"Who guides you?"

"A higher being, an intermediary between this planet and other planets."

"Have you ever seen this individual?"

"Only as a light, not in form."

"What exactly do you do for those seeking your advice professionally?" I asked.

"I work out of the Tzaddi Creative Center in Garden Grove, and we have a chartered organization there, counseling and doing ministerial work."

After some further discussion, I established that Mr. Wagner considered himself a medium and that he believed that he was able to communicate with the dead. As an example, he said: "My wife's first husband came through and gave us actual tangible evidence at one of their anniversaries by materializing an orange bag of rice. They had painted their ceiling orange when they first got married, so that was quite symbolic. He disappeared after it had been materialized." Mr. Wagner, who had some difficulty coming to the point, then explained that he had been in trance at times, and said things that he couldn't possibly have known. On one occasion he spoke Spanish, which he does not know, and acted the role of a Mexican priest. As such, he was recognized by someone who had known the priest in his lifetime. He readily offered some testimonials about his work: "I feel that today's going to change my whole life and that Leo Wagner has done it all.

R. C." In a test undertaken by editors Richard Bacon and Tom Valentine, the newsweekly *The National Tattler* confirmed that Leo Wagner came through with flying colors. In December, 1972, Valentine asked Wagner to send the newspaper a letter predicting what subjects would be dealt with in their January 7, 1973, issue. The issue had already been written and planned but had not yet been printed. Wagner apparently sat down immediately and wrote a letter, which arrived at the *Tattler* office in Chicago on December 15, 1972. Evidently Leo Wagner scored well, whether by reading the thoughts of the two editors or by using his ability of precognition.

The trouble with Mr. Wagner is that he does so many things, or claims to be able to, that the abilities he really possesses get drowned in the flash flood of claims. He believes he is related to the composer Richard Wagner, blissfully ignoring the fact that Wagner is one of the most common German names. Originally he did special police work for the city of Los Angeles. Later, he worked as an operating engineer in a power house for United States Steel, and after thirty years of doing this he retired. He brings a certain naiveté to his new profession. When I asked him when he started to work professionally, he replied, "What lifetime do you mean?"

It appears that Mr. Wagner had shown an interest in psychic phenomena since age fourteen but made it his full-time occupation only after his retirement. He advertises himself as "ESP researcher," although he does no ESP research. He is married, and his children are all grown up. The La Habra section of the *Los Angeles News—Tribune* carried Mr. Wagner's predictions for 1973 early that year. Out of some twenty predictions, only one has so far come true, but it would not really matter since most of them were couched in such vague language that their realization could hardly be meaningful. In this respect, Mr. Wagner is no better or worse than other psychics, some with far bigger reputations, who predict future events in the January issues of popular newspapers. I asked Leo Wagner to get "into my vibration," and see whether he received any impression about my own future. After closing his eyes and going through a religious prayer, Leo Wagner informed me that I would be getting an important call having to do with Vienna. He also stated that I would be doing some motion picture work, and something that I hadn't gotten into before. "The motion picture *The Exorcist* is going to spiral some new investigations concerning exorcism, and there will be a demand to know." He also stated that the name Kelly would have some connection with me. This was on December 10, 1973; in March, 1974, I received a proposition about motion picture work involving Vienna, and about the same time had a number of discussions with a newspaper editor named Kelly concerning a possible column. Certainly, Mr. Wagner could not have guessed this from what is known about me.

Leo Wagner says he does not charge for his services but accepts free will offerings, which are expected to be somewhere between five and ten dollars for half an hour's work. Those who wish to avail themselves of his services may reach Leo Wagner at: 11236 Dale Street, Garden Grove, California 92641; or at his home, 2051 Monte Vista Street, La Habra, California 90631. Telephone: 805-697-9625. **No comment.**

In the Long Beach area, Reverend Bob Bourcier is available for private readings and also teaches classes in spiritual development. He conducts a Saturday night service and may be reached at: 5370 Olive Avenue, Long Beach, California 90805. Telephone: 213-GA3-6955. **No comment.**

Up near San Francisco, there is a young woman with a long string of psychic experiences in her life. I've written of her in *Ghosts of the Golden West* and met her time and again as her spiritual development brought her to the point of deciding to become a professional psychic. Because of her own experiences she has learned to be cautious in the acceptance of phenomena, thus she tends to be just as cautious in her readings. Known as Jean to her friends, the Reverend Phaetyn E. Grasso can be reached at: 1017½ Capuchino Avenue, Burlingame, California 94010. **Recommended.**

In Redlands, psychic Fred Andrews enjoys somewhat of a reputation with his readings. Those wishing to test his skill may reach him at: Creative Living, Inc., 16 East Fern Avenue, Redlands, California 92373. Telephone: 714-792-1150. **Satisfactory.**

Reverend Katharine Sweet practices her Spiritualist mediumship at the Abundant Life Church of Jesus Christ, Inc., at 7487 Elm Street, San Bernardino, California 92410. Telephone: 714-889-3340. In San Diego, Reverend Betty Voss has acquired somewhat of a reputation as a Spiritualist medium and teacher of spiritual unfoldment. She may be reached at: 4031 Idaho Street, San Diego, California 92104. Telephone: 714-296-3555. **Satisfactory.**

It seems strange that San Francisco, despite its great interest in occult matters, does not have a really great psychic living in the city. Ever since Flora Becker passed away, no one has yet come forward to take her place. However, the Metaphysical Townhall Bookshop is a center of information and might be helpful locating satisfactory psychics in the area. Address: 345 Mason Street, San Francisco, California 94102.

There are many fine astrologers in California. Foremost is Sidney Omarr, a prolific writer on the subject, with his own syndicated news column and radio show, a man who has practiced astrology as a professional and full-time occupation for many years. Sidney Omarr is a technician who takes his craft very seriously. He is about as far removed from the two-bit astrology columns written by some semipros that appear in many local newspapers as Albert Einstein was from the high school student just barely making it in math. Even his popular columns are informative and no exaggerated claims are made. Despite his public activities, Omarr does individual charts. Those wishing to contact him should write to: Sidney Omarr, 232 Alcyona Drive, Los Angeles, California 90068. **Recommended.**

Virginia O'Hallahan, known to her friends as Gitana, the Gypsy, is a spunky Irish lady who has been an astrologer for many years. Although she bases her charts on mathematical calculations, as any good astrologer does, she has had proof of her own psychic talents over the years, and therefore her interpretations of individual horoscopes are sometimes far deeper and more elaborate than those of other astrologers not so gifted. The cost of her charts runs from thirty-five dollars and up, depending upon the extent of each service requested. Those who wish to get in touch with her can reach her at: 992 Trinity Avenue, Seaside, California 93955. **Recommended.**

Victoria Saint Cyr neither looks nor acts like the conventional astrologer, which is not surprising since she became involved in professional astrology only six years ago. Prior to that time, she worked as a secretary and also did some modeling in the field of television commercials. Through a psychic friend, Virginia Maxwell, she became involved with the occult, and astrology in particular, and eventually took classes to perfect herself as an astrologer. She studied with Angela Louise Gallo and Dr. Zipporah Dobyns for a period of three years. After that, she began to set up in business as a professional astrologer. "I've done President Nixon's chart for which I received a letter from him," the tall, dark-haired Victoria explained. "I've done charts for many executives of well-known industrial companies such as Stephen Ross of Warner Brothers and many more."

Miss Saint Cyr does not specialize in any particular aspect of astrology, but she has been successful with stock market charts and general astrology. She charges $125.00 for a chart. "I combine numerology with astrology," she explained. "I set up two charts and then compare them with each other. One chart is always backed up by the other." Those wishing to reach Miss Victoria Saint Cyr, may write: 438½ Landfair Avenue, Los Angeles, California 90024. **Recommended.**

One of the best astrologers around, and a nice person to chat with, is Betty Collins, who lives in a picturesque little house of considerable antiquity in Hollywood. Miss Collins's clients include many actors and actresses as well as business people. She maintains charts and counsels her clients from time to time, referring to her records. I hate to call her an "old pro," since she is not that advanced in years, but the interpretation she gave me based upon studying my chart was quite accurate and more than satisfactory in terms of details. Those wishing to contact Betty Collins will find her at: 1631 North Genesee, Hollywood, California 90046. Telephone: 213-874-4457. **Recommended.**

In the Long Beach area, Will Canady gives astrological readings and lessons. He may be reached through Solomon's Shop Of The Occult Mysteries: 73A Atlantic, Long Beach, California 90802. Telephone: 213-437-4511. **No comment.**

A rather offbeat practitioner of the occult arts is Grace Emerson, who used the "Divine Quabala" as her source of information. She does charts for individuals using certain principles of numerology along with metaphysical concepts. Her charts consist of four parts: Birth Path, Material, Divinity, and Total. The "Birth Path" shows on what level one is, according to Miss Emerson, and it influences the entire life. The "Material" evaluates the name of the client in terms of the Quabala and represents the outside world and guidance on a professional level. "Divinity" has to do with health and love life, and "Total" addresses itself to the numbers obtained from the other three departments. Miss Emerson lives in a small, aged house, her study is a metaphysical retreat, and Miss Emerson herself is a gracious lady in her middle years, pursuing an essentially religiously accented career. She has written a pamphlet called "The Thought Computer," which she calls a key to mental control. When I met her, I gave her my birth date and asked her for an interpretation. As a result she handed me a carefully typed little booklet, containing in some twenty pages all there was about me, my life, and my expectations. There are a number of statements in this reading I found interesting and evidential. "In this lifetime you could be a great collector of paintings or art objects." I collect art objects and like paintings. "Your number can have a negative side, since you are a giver you can overdo things and in so doing you take away the individuality of the other person." I've often been accused of trying to do too much for others. "From 1935 to 1942 you could have got a scholarship in some field." It was in 1939 that I was offered a scholarship to Haverford, but declined for personal reasons. Those wishing to get a reading from numerologist Grace Emerson, may contact her at: 9261¼ Burton Way, Beverly Hills, California 90210. **Satisfactory.**

Lynn Cameron bills herself as a Certified Grapho Analyst, and those wishing to avail themselves of her services in graphology can reach her at 213-242-1212 in the Los Angeles area. **Satisfactory.**

Arden D. Zimmerman is not an occultist in the narrow sense of the term, but the creator and developer of the Specific Adjusting Machine, a device combining Chiropractic principles with instruments devised to make the effort safer and less dependent upon the individual practitioner. Those wishing to obtain additional information should contact Dr. Zimmerman directly at: 1650 The Alameda, San Jose, California 95126. Telephone: 408-293-5360. **Satisfactory.**

Finally, anyone in need of a hypnotist might find the two

listings that follow of use. Robert J. Strong is a hypnotist with an active interest in parapsychology and also teaches self-hypnosis. He may be reached at: 13648 Danbrook Drive, Whittier, California 90605. Telephone: 213-693-2321. On the theatrical end of the scale, well-known stage hypnotist Pat Collins, who owns a night club in Hollywood, may be reached at: Route 1, Box 342-A, Fair Haven, Maryland 20754. Telephone: 301-257-7700. **Satisfactory.**

District of Columbia

Psychic Observer, the erstwhile Spiritualist journal prominent in the field in the 1950s and early 1960s until the Spiritualist camp scandals destroyed it, is now being published in smaller form by the Reverend Diane S. Negorka with her husband. Mrs. Negorka is also the Pastor of the First Spiritual Church of Washington, D.C., Inc. Although she is a reputable Spiritualist minister, the journal itself is somewhat on the naive side, but very useful. Both can be contacted at: 5605 Sixteenth Street, N.W., Washington, D.C. 20011. Telephone: 202-723-4578. **Satisfactory.**

Eileen Culkin is a Scorpio, and perhaps because of it an extremely intuitive astrologer. She does charts at thirty-five dollars. Address: 6101 Kirby Road, Bethesda, Maryland 20034. **Recommended.**

Reverend Theodore Swager has acquired a good reputation as a clairvoyant and spiritualist medium. He may be reached at: Route 1, Box 342-A, Fair Haven, Maryland 20754. Telephone: 301-257-7700. **Satisfactory.**

Florida

I have already mentioned the organization headed by Reverend Noel Street in Miami. Noel Street himself is a capable clairvoyant and trance medium and may be reached at: 128 North East, Eighty-second Terrace, Miami, Florida 33138. **Satisfactory.**

One of the newer mediums who has recently come into prominence is Mrs. Judith Laurie, who has had some remarkable impressions concerning the Flagler Mansion ghost, and has on occasion had visions of future events that could be verified factually. Mrs. Laurie may be reached by correspondence at: 122 West Thirty-fifth Street, Riviera Beach, Florida 33404. **Recommended.**

Georgia

In Atlanta, the most reputable organization is the already mentioned Metaphysical Center headed by Reverend and Mrs. Peter Calhoun. In addition, Anita Josey, instructor in psychic awareness at Oglethorpe University, is active in the field. Individual practitioners include: the Reverend Paul Neary, a psychic who may be reached at 404-233-8141 in Atlanta; the Reverend Robert Goodman, at 404-688-6174, also in Atlanta; and astrologer Maxine Taylor, 2345 South Four Lane Highway, Smyna, Georgia 30080, telephone 404-636-8197; and Midge Kraus, essentially a supplier of astrological books at 6130 Roswell Road, N.E., Atlanta, Georgia 30328. Mrs. Myrna Bentley is an established graphologist and can be reached at: 475 Bridges Creek Trail, N.E., Atlanta, Georgia 30328. Telephone: 404-255-0667. Ben Osborne, psychic and teacher, may be reached at: Post Office Box 13361, Atlanta, Georgia 30324. Telephone: 404-876-3553. These individuals range from **satisfactory** to **no comment.**

Betty Dye, praised by me as a remarkable healer in *Beyond Medicine*, is also an equally astounding medium. She has the ability of clairvoyance, psychic photography, and spirit communication, and shows significant talents in each area. Although her healing ability has recently drawn the majority of her clients, she gives private sittings by arrangement at her home near Atlanta. Those wishing to see her should make inquiries as to the fee for each sitter. Healing sittings are fifty dollars per person. Address: Post Office Box 82687, Hapeville, Georgia 30354. **Recommended.**

Illinois

Chicago is one of the chief centers of psychic activities in the United States. The number of professionals resident in and around Chicago is considerable, but the number I am able to list here is very small simply because I have not been able to check out more than a portion of those working in the area. At the top of the list must of necessity by Irene Hughes, whom I have known for many years, and who has accompanied me on an evidential ghost hunt long before Brad Steiger decided to do the same with her and record his impressions in a book called *Irene Hughes on Psychic Safari*. Irene Hughes has also written a book of her own called *ESPecially Irene*, with the first three letters capitalized to indicate somewhat obviously her connection with ESP. Mrs. Hughes has had the gift of second sight from early childhood, was born and raised in the South, and comes from a Scottish Indian heritage. The last time we met at her spanking new offices in one of Chicago's skyscrapers, and then over lunch, I asked her to define how she viewed her life's work at the present time, after having been so very successful as a clairvoyant, medium, radio and television guest, and lecturer; in short, the leading medium in the Midwest.

"It is my life's work," the quiet, soft-spoken Irene explained. "The only thing I would like to do more of is solving crimes and perhaps doing more work in the healing area. I wish there were an academy of police in psychics. For many years I have tried to form an organization whereby psychics who received warnings of impending crimes or disasters would put their knowledge to good use."

"Apart from your nationally known predictions and your work with the police, how do you categorize the service you perform for individuals?"

"I feel psychic counseling is very important," Irene Hughes replied. "It involves business people, professionals, politicians, and I do this here or away from the office. I do not involve my psychic impressions with my work in astrology, even though I often say, 'What is your birth date?' There is a reason for that. When I first started out, I was a Southern Baptist, and I felt everything I did should begin with prayer. Some people objected to this, since they were of different faiths, so I eventually substituted the query for the birth date."

Irene Hughes has two careers, one as a psychic, and one as an astrologer. She keeps them as separate as possible, so that clients may contact her for either or both of these services. For several years she worked primarily as a trance medium, later she went away from it and concentrated more on counseling, but she says she uses spirit communication in her work. She is controlled by what she calls a "spirit teacher," though she will not divulge his name. Her sittings take half an hour. Generally, she covers both personal life and business life for her clients. Sometimes she involves herself in medical projects and healing as well. She has on a number of occasions worked with medical doctors, without ever meeting or seeing the patient for whom she gives a diagnosis. All this is done through the mail; at present she does not administer healing directly. In 1967 someone suggested she become an astrologer, and at first she rejected the notion. Eventually she changed her mind and studied under Norman Aarons, ennabling her to teach a course in astrology herself at a community college for three semesters. It helped her understand herself and others a lot better, though in interpreting charts she draws for her clients, she tries to stick strictly to astrological concepts. "However, if something is revealed to me psychically, I then say this is a psychic impression above and beyond the mathematical calculations in your chart, for I feel that being a psychic helps me to see more deeply different meanings."

Irene Hughes also gives readings by mail, probably one of the few reputable psychics who do. She is able to do this since she is very good at psychometry. That is how she works in police cases. For instance, someone gives her an object from a murdered individual, and she tries to get an impression of the crime. She does accept new clients both for her psychic work and as an astrologer. However, many of those wishing personal interviews may have to wait as much as several months until she can clear the time for them. Her office is staffed by two full-time assistants and a secretary. She also does a syndicated newspaper column and is planning to write more books about her work.

The list of her public predictions, especially about headline-making figures is impressive; that is to say those that actually came true as made. She predicted Vice-President Agnew's downfall, due to legal problems, and has Bob Kennedy, the Chicago talk show host, as a witness. Earlier, Mrs. Hughes had accurately predicted the assassination of both John F. and Robert Kennedy, the outbreak of the 1967 Near Eastern war, and the remarriage of Jacqueline Kennedy.

Those wishing to contact Irene Hughes may reach her at: 500 North Michigan Avenue, Suite 1040, Chicago, Illinois 60611. Telephone: 312-467-1140. **Recommended.**

Harriet Manuel is a gentle, conscientious black medium who first came to see me in 1969 while she was living in New York City. At the time she gave me a remarkably accurate reading, citing several of my dead relatives by name, and making predictions about my future that are only now coming true. She spoke of a conductor of music in my family, of my own involvement in music in the future, of my signing to make a movie, and of living on an estate in Austria. She mentioned my late mother, Martha, by name, and described my father-in-law both by appearance and background. None of this information could have been available to her at the time she gave the reading in September of 1969. All of what she said was correct. A year later I asked Harriet Manuel to accompany me on a ghost hunt in Chicago, in conjunction with Bob Kennedy and a film crew. That, too, proved to be extremely evidential. Harriet Manuel gives private readings and may be reached at: 4518 Forestville, Chicago, Illinois 60657. Telephone: 312-546-5206. She may have moved since giving me this address. **Recommended.**

Henry Rucker, black healer and occult teacher, discovered his psychic gifts when he was only eight years old. He was able to "hear" the thoughts of people in the room, and after a few years of this, to tell people what would happen to them in the future. His fortune-telling ability surprised him, but after holding down a variety of uninteresting jobs, ranging from sales positions to postal clerk, he decided to concentrate on psychic work full time. He has lectured at various area colleges, and functions as a psychic healer. However, he is available for general psychic reading at his headquarters in Chicago. His is probably the only psychic research foundation headed by a black man. Address: 192 North Clark Street, Chicago, Illinois 60601. **Recommended.**

Paranormal analysis was the name of the game when I first heard of Penny South. She had developed a particular ability to get psychic impressions from the handwriting of those who came to consult her. Eventually, she discovered that she also had the gift of trance mediumship and offered her services to me in some of my investigations. I sat with her a number of times, took her to allegedly haunted houses, and found her to be extremely disciplined and knowledgeable. At the time, she was married to a Chicago policeman and had to overcome his natural skepticism concerning her talents. It is to his and her eternal credit that they were able to see eye to eye on the importance of her work. A little later, Penny South founded the Society of Psychic Awareness and Research with herself as the first president. She managed to rally around her in sub-urban Chicago a number of local psychics and lecturers and to carry on a lively pop-style educational program covering all phases of the occult. She began to publish a newsletter and to appear on various television interview programs. The address for the society is: 1120 South Mayfield Avenue, Chicago, Illinois 60644. Membership dues are a few dollars and well worth it. The society holds meetings once a month in which a guest speaker talks on some phase of psychic and occult phenomena. Once yearly, a special retreat is offered by the society for all members for the sole purpose of developing and enriching their sixth senses. Free development classes are part of the society's activities, and Penny South lets prospective members know that she means business. "The only stipulation is that you attend each meeting or not miss more than three meetings in a row or your name will be stricken from the membership list." Today, Penny South is probably the second best known psychic in the state of Illinois. Those wishing to book private readings with her or to engage her in some quasi-public activity, should contact her via correspondence at: Penny South, 9235 West Capitol Drive, Milwaukee, Wisconsin. Telephone: 414-463-7482. **Recommended.**

Aquarian Clifford Royce is at the head of a center calling itself the Chicago Psychic Center, Inc., although it is located in Oak Park, a suburb. Mr. Royce sponsors lectures and demonstrations by other psychics, makes annual predictions for various newspapers, and is an amiable fellow all around. This, despite the fact that not many of his annual predictions come true as made. Mr. Royce is a practical man, professional in every sense of the word, and gives private consultations. Those wishing to book with him should contact him at: The Chicago Psychic Center, Inc., 451 West South Boulevard, Oak

Park, Illinois 60302. Telephone: 312-848-8522. **Satisfactory.**

Self-styled "noted psychic" Milton Kramer also has acquired some reputation as an accurate forecaster of future
events, especially to area newspapers. Mr. Kramer can be
contacted for private readings at: 4539 West Howard, Skokie,
Illinois 60076. Telephone: 312-679-4398. **Satisfactory.**

Former Hair Salon owner Joseph De Luise has managed to
parlay a remarkable prediction concerning a bridge disaster in
Ohio into a successful career as a major psychic. Mr. De
Luise is extremely publicity minded, lectures publicly, and has
a large following in the Midwest. I met and interviewed Mr.
De Luise several years ago and found him a fascinating man
whose psychic ability goes back into his childhood, as with so
many mediums. The bridge disaster in Ohio was by no means
the only thing he predicted in detail long before it occurred,
and there can be no doubt that he has the gift of clairvoyance.
He is on less sure ground when trying to explain some of the
phenomena that had best be explained by scientists in the
field. Those wishing to book a session with the personable Mr.
De Luise may reach him at 312-782-3166 in Chicago, Illinois.
Satisfactory.

Reverend Orchid E. Neal, spiritualist minister and reader,
seems to be in the process of getting better known in the
immediate Chicago area. The Reverend Neal may be contacted at: 833 South Humphrey, Oak Park, Illinois 60304.
Telephone: 312-383-2002. **No comment.**

Mary Anne is the name for an astrologer specializing in
compatibility charts, that is astrological evaluation of the
common bonds between married couples or men and women
interested in each other. However, Mary Anne also does
general and business charts. She may be contacted at: North
Avenue at Bloomingdale, Glen Ellyn, Illinois. Telephone:
312-665-6015. **Recommended.**

Although it is a little publicized and certainly minor part of his activities, Frederico de Arechaga, head and spiritual leader of the Sabaean Society of Chicago, also engages in special consultations, in which he uses his not inconsiderable amount of psychic ability to help people. On one occasion at least, he was able to locate a missing child for the distraught parent; on other occasions he was able to accurately forecast future events for private clients. Although Mr. de Arechaga would be the last to consider himself a medium, he nevertheless is a first-rate psychic, and those lucky enough to get a sitting with him will find their time spent excitingly and usefully. In addition to his priestly duties at the temple of the Sabaeans, Mr. de Arechaga operates an occult shop called El Sabarum at 2553 North Halsted, Chicago, Illinois 60614, and it is there that inquiries concerning possible sittings should be directed. **Recommended.**

Indiana

Madeline Sandfur is not only a peculiar name (it is actually a pseudonym), but it belongs to a most unusual person. Madeline is a grandmother, albeit a youngish one, who has discovered hidden psychic talents in herself and combined them with more obvious physical talents—viz, body massage. When I met her at the Hampshire House in Chicago, Madeline emphasized that it was her belief that much of the illness in this world was caused by sexual hangups, which led her into the direction of applying her two talents together in a way that would make life easier for a lot of seekers.

"I am teaching men to respond spontaneously, mentally, sexually, emotionally, without conflict with their normal natural impulses, without religious hang-ups and confusions."

"But how would you describe the kind of work you do in simple terms?"

"I am a psychic masseuse."

Individual Practitioners 87

"How did you get into this line of work?"

"I come from a small town, went to school at age five, and finished high school. For a while I worked in a factory, then I got married and had three children. Later I went back to work in sewing factories and eventually divorced my husband. All my children are married. Fifteen years ago, I became interested in the work of Edgar Cayce and went to Virginia Beach where I learned about diet and yoga. When I returned to the Middle West, I tried to apply what I had learned to my way of life. I met a chiropractor and masseur, Dr. Harold Beck, who believed in natural treatment, and through his massages my state of health improved rapidly."

"Then what made you decide to become a professional psychic masseuse?"

"Nine years ago a psychic told me I would be doing healing work with my hands, but it actually won't be *your* hands that would do it. Actually, the spirit is flowing through me when I work now. Somehow I was led to a massage parlor where I worked for a couple of months, and that was the beginning. I gave massages to both men and women, and soon people said I did something for them that others didn't do. The result was—people were getting healings from my massages. A man who hadn't been able to walk well for fifteen years and had gone to every specialist he could find, got two massages from me, and as a result, walked for five miles without trouble. When I healed him, there were lights flashing all around his body. I was not the only one who saw it."

"Did other masseuses have similar results with their clients?"

"No. Even the man who ran the place, and he was a tremendous masseur, did not get these kinds of results."

"Then what is this *extra* that you put into your work?"

"I can't name it, except that it just flows through me and whatever the person on the table needs, he gets."

"What did your boss say about it?"

"He was absolutely dumbfounded, saying she does every-thing wrong, and yet she gets the right results. I stayed there for two months, but then everybody wanted me to come to their own place to give them a massage, or to come to my home. So I did, and I've never worked publicly since then. Most of the time, people come to my house, and I've been doing this for nine years now. People come to me regularly because I free them from whatever is holding them back from being what they want to be. I set them free through my awareness."

"Do you manipulate your clients the way a chiropractor does?"

"If this is indicated, otherwise I just massage. There is no special manipulation, no special technique. My intuition tells me what particular area needs to be worked on to break loose a person's rigidity, and when that area relaxes, the electric current, which is a portion of the soul, will flow through my fingers. I will pick up what a person is expressing, and when it reaches my mind, the customer may feel something revealing a memory of what I am already picking up in my own mind. That is how I know I am doing the right thing."

Madeline only accepts new clients if they are referred to her by someone she already knows. Since she is not technically licensed to do this work, Madeline does not want to get into any kind of legal trouble. Her fee is only ten dollars, and she spends about half an hour with each client. She does not guarantee any results, only a good massage. "The result depends on the person's response to me, and everybody doesn't respond. A person may come to me for six months and may just be getting a good massage, and then one day some-thing hits him and there is a change."

Those who wish to put their case before her, in the hope that she may take them on as clients, can write to: Madeline Sandfur, Post Office Box 25, Evansville, Indiana 47701. **Satisfactory.**

Robert Carmack not only advertises the fact that he was born under the Leo-Virgo cusp, but also offers to do spiritual readings, card readings, and general mediumistic consultations. Mr Carmack may be reached at: 101 East Tennessee, Evansville, Indiana 47711. Telephone: 812-422-9114. **No comment.**

Iowa

A few years ago, medium Shawn Robbins of New York City brought a young midwestern astrologer to my attention, who immediately impressed me by the accuracy of his work and the reasonableness of his outlook. Gar Osten is probably the most promising young astrologer in the United States today. Solidly footed in conventional astrology, he knows his craft and how to cast horoscopes, even the more complicated charts called progressions as well as various specialty charts. He is also quite psychic and combines his psychic insight with his astrological knowledge.

"I do individual charts, erecting and interpreting horoscopes from the date, hour, and place of birth. The client gets a birth chart, my typewritten analysis (usually covering between fifteen and twenty pages), and progressions for most of the life and predictions. The fee for this is twenty-five dollars. Also, I do work investigating missing persons or unusual deaths, and the fee for this is the same. I require birth data, as completely as possible on all individuals involved in such cases, the date of the disappearance or death, and the time, if known. The client receives charts for the individual, a typewritten analysis of what is likely to have occurred, and what the outlook and timing of future dates will be. I also do yearly forecasts, and this only for the year in question, and I prefer to work from birthday to birthday. The fee is twenty dollars, and the analysis will usually cover anywhere from ten to fifteen pages."

Mr. Osten can be reached by mail at: 315 South Third Avenue East, Newton, Iowa 50208. **Recommended.**

Kansas

If you are interested in whatever happened to St. Anthony of Padua, the wife of St. Peter, Mary Baker Eddy, or Louis XIV, perhaps Helen L. Hall of Hutchinson, Kansas, has the answer for you. Helen L. Hall is the author of "The Drama of Rebirth: A Study of Reincarnational Patterns," and those fascinated by this (fictional undoubtedly) account of some celebrated historical figures, may contact Miss Hall at: Route #1, Hutchinson, Kansas 67501. It may just be that *you* figure in there somewhere. **No comment.**

Louisiana

Although there are a number of Creole soothsayers in ole New Orleans, the one person whose integrity I can vouch for is Ron Warmoth, a favorite of Hollywood actors and actresses, formerly a resident of New York City. I first met Mr. Warmoth in November, 1970, in New York. At that time he was teaching at the Wainwright House in Rye, New York, and had been very much interested in working with teenagers and drug addicts, trying to adjust them to society. He had originally contacted me after reading my book on reincarnation, *Born Again*, as a result of which I had a sitting with him at his home on New York's East Side. Although I had come alone for the reading, Mr. Warmoth correctly diagnosed a "stomach condition" around my wife as a pregnancy and felt that we would be in Austria at the time the child was due. As a matter of fact, the child was born in April, and we left for Austria in early July. He also saw me writing a biography, a genealogy of a family, documented and elaborated upon. At that time, *The Habsburg Curse* had not yet been written. He saw me writing fictional books, something that is more and more becoming of interest to me now. He saw me going to England in connection with the writing of a book. At the time of this prediction, the idea of writing *The Great British Ghost Hunt* had not yet entered my mind. He described a home in Europe where I would live part time, close to a mountainous area. "On a rise, like the foothills of a mountain, but it is in a valley with mountains on both sides, and then a clear spot where you could see a good long ways. The valley runs north and south." A more perfect description of our house in Austria could not have been made if Mr. Warmoth had been to the house, which of course he hadn't. But the prediction that made the shivers run up my spine, concerning a future television series of mine, was given on November 15, 1970. "It will be a large corporation, something to do with household items. I am picking up something to do with the word lever." As I write these very lines, a large New York advertising agency is pitching my television series to one of their clients, Lever Brothers. I do not know the outcome, but the fact is, it is being discussed. How could Warmoth have known this four years before?

Those wishing to contact Ron Warmoth may reach him at: 97 Rue St. Anne, New Orleans, Louisiana. **Recommended.**

Missouri

In the St. Louis area Beverly C. Jaegers has gained somewhat of a reputation as a psychic and clairvoyant. She also arranges for development classes and lectures and has worked with local law enforcement authorities. Miss Jaegers may be reached at: Post Office Box 9226, Richmond Heights, Missouri 63117. Telephone: 314-647-4398. **No comment.**

Mrs. Sybil Leek, a close friend and associate, runs a School of Astrology in St. Louis, Missouri, in conjunction with the Theosophical Lodge of that city. Mrs. Leek is one of the world's best trance mediums, but does her work in this respect exclusively for scientific purposes, and has in the past worked with me on a number of important projects, many of which I have published in my books. She does not give private readings as commercial professionals do. However, she is also a superb astrologer and does charts for individuals by correspondence. Letters addressed to Mrs. Sybil Leek containing a stamped forwarding envelope, will be forwarded by her publisher, Stein & Day, Scarborough House, Briarcliff Manor, New York, New York 10510. **Recommended.**

New Jersey

Penny Sarama conducts seances from time to time and gives private psychic readings. She also helps the police in some cases involving murders or missing persons. However, she does not like to give worldwide predictions, as other mediums do. She works either from her home or goes to a client's house. Those wishing to contact Mrs. Sarama for a reading should write to: 24 Brandywine Drive, Berlin, New Jersey 08009. **No comment.**

New York

In New York City, the number one medium is, and has been for many years, Ethel Johnson Meyers. I have written of her many times in my books, because she was the first trance medium I worked with who has come with me into many haunted houses and helped me lay the ghosts. We met in the 1950s at the headquarters of the Association for Research and Enlightenment, or Cayce Foundation, on West Sixteenth Street in New York City. At that time, Mrs. Meyers was trying to develop her mediumship strictly on a part-time basis, her main occupation being that of a vocal coach and teacher. Mrs. Meyers' career had been a long and honorable one, first as an opera singer with the San Francisco Opera Company, later still, as a singer in vaudeville together with her first husband, a musician named Albert, who eventually became her spirit guide. When we met, I was immediately impressed by Ethel's sincerity and level-headed approach to the phenomena with which she was involved. In those days, in the early 1950s, there were a number of potential mediums around, eager to experiment with researchers like myself. Another one, whom I met at the same time, was the late Betty Ritter. Shortly after our meeting, Ethel Meyers consented to accompany a group of researchers, including myself, to a haunted house on Fifth Avenue, New York, and from that grew a six-month investigation described in my first book, *Ghost Hunter*, as the Fifth Avenue ghost. Hundreds upon hundreds of investigations followed throughout the years, and when I moved to Seventieth Street, where I had a large apartment, I began regular weekly circles with Ethel as the medium. These sessions were free to interested individuals and yielded much valuable information. They were not exactly Spiritualist seances, but open-minded research sessions in which anything could happen. I was pretty severe in those days as far as evidence was concerned, and at times came into conflict with the esoteric spirit masters speaking through Ethel when she was in trance. On the other hand, there were exciting sessions, such as the one in which the renowned astrologer Charles Jayne spoke to a deceased Indian astrologer who used such technical terms that even he had to look things up *afterwards*. As a result of this extraordinary trance contact, Mr. Jayne was able to calculate the orbits of two as yet undiscovered planets in our solar system. Mrs. Meyers was not always successful in giving evidence to the degree I demanded it, but she was more often right than not, more often accurate in her predictions and clairvoyance, and at no time attempted to say things that did not come to her directly from the primary source. When the volume of material coming through Ethel Meyers became so large that I could no longer handle it alone, I applied to Eileen Garrett and the Parapsychology Foundation for help. The late Eileen Garrett arranged for transcriptions to be made, equipment to be lent to me, because in those days I didn't even own a tape recorder. The results of several years' work eventually were incorporated into a scientific report to the Foundation as well as my first book *Ghost Hunter*. In addition to expeditions to haunted houses, we concentrated on evidence for communication with the so-called dead, and we received plenty. One of those taking part in the early sessions was Bernard Axelrod of the *New York Daily News*, a friendly if skeptical observer. Others included the equally skeptical painter, Jan de Ruth; the late Victor Sifton, head of the Psychical Research Society in Manitoba, Canada; former *Harper's Bazaar* astrologer, Xavora Pove; Fawcett editor, Adolph Barreaux; my attorney, Carl Blank; and various other interested people.

Ethel became a medium by accident, not by design. She was skeptical herself, even though she noticed the ability to foresee events at an early age. But her career was firmly footed in the theater, and she paid no particular attention to phenomena that did not seem to belong on the stage. When her first husband passed away unexpectedly and far too soon, she was very distraught. In her depressed state, she was talked into visiting a number of psychics in the hope that there might be some sort of communication, or at the very least, some counsel for herself. At that point, she was not a believer but felt she had nothing to lose by consulting the mediums her friends suggested. Being a medium herself was the furthest thing from her mind. Apparently, the results were not satisfactory because Ethel began to think of doing away with herself, unable to go on alone. On one particular day, when she was especially despondent, her first husband appeared to her surrounded by a strange light and warned her not to commit suicide. From then on, Ethel took an interest in the occult, began to read and talk to others active in the field, and no longer suppressed her own incipient mediumship. As the years went on, it became clear to her that she was one of the chosen ones who could bring the dead in contact with the living. Still cautious in accepting things, especially when they came from her, she nevertheless realized that she had a special gift and decided to investigate it. When an opportunity presented itself to sit at the Association for Research and Enlightenment, she took it, and eventually we met.

Partially through my books, partially through word of mouth, her fame spread to the point at which strangers sought her out for sittings. It became impossible for her to carry on a quiet career as a vocal coach and singing teacher, and she began to do professional readings for people recommended to her. As yet, she pursued a double career; some very famous actors and singers came to her for classes, only to discover that their singing teacher was also a medium. In the case of Larry Blyden, this was particularly fortunate since he lived in a haunted house in New Jersey. With my help, the house was investigated and a seance held that dislodged the ghost, who had been one of the original owners way back in the eighteenth century. Her second husband, Daniel, at first took no part in Ethel's expanding interest in the occult. But as the years went on, he became fascinated by her work and moved closer to her philosophy. The Meyers built a house in the mountains of Connecticut, and soon Ethel divided her week between Connecticut and New York City, as a result of which she could no longer carry on a double career. Although she still teaches an occasional lesson, especially to her old clients, she has for the past few years been exclusively a professional medium, giving sittings by appointment and working with scientists such as myself, Dr. Karlis Osis of the American Society for Psychical Research, Ray van Over of Hoeffstra College, and others. Her trance work, especially deep trance, Ethel reserves for scientific investigations as she feels more comfortable doing it in the presence of an expert who can get her out of an unwanted trance, should that ever be the case. When she and I visited the town house of the late financier Serge Rubinstein, she was possessed by the restless spirit of the murdered financier, and as a result, I had somewhat of a troubled time dislodging the possessing entity from Mrs. Meyers's body. Deep trance experiments should never be undertaken except by experts who know how to break the trance state, should there be an emergency.

People write to Ethel for appointments way ahead, because it may take as much as two or three months before she can fit them into her schedule. Of course, if a real emergency exists or a life is at stake, there is always a way of breaking through the time barrier. Because of her generous nature, Mrs. Meyers had to learn to apportion her time and to restrict her sittings to no more than an hour at a time. As most reputable mediums do, she refuses to give readings by mail or telephone, but she welcomes an object belonging to the person to be read, since psychometry can be a valuable inducing agent to deepen the perception. On more than one occasion when I have worked with her, she has spoken in a language she would not normally speak, such as Ketchua, a South American Indian dialect. Frequently, deceased family members of mine have spoken through her, leaving no doubt in my mind that they were indeed who they claimed to be. When I researched a book about the late Bishop James Pike, the bishop himself spoke to me through Ethel in a dramatic finale to my investigation using phraseology and even the movement of hands I remembered clearly from my extended contact with him during his lifetime. Once in a while, someone asks for Mrs. Meyers's services, and she finds she cannot read him or her because of a block or some sort of malfunction in the communication system between client and medium. In such cases, she has always refused to try, knowing so well that she will not be able to do a satisfactory job.

Despite one or two incidents of police harassment in the early years, Mrs. Meyers has steadfastly refused to take cover under a "reverend" designation, thus assuming the mantle of the spiritual minister that New York State law seems to require for psychics. The harassment, which was merely one of inquiry, had been initiated by an eager policewoman looking for credits, and was quickly disposed of when the real nature of the setup became known. Ethel Meyers has never made any claim, other than giving her time for which she is being paid, guaranteeing nothing more than an effort to give her clients a satisfactory reading, or, if that should happen, a reliable and evidential contact with a dead relative.

Mrs. Meyers has two spirit controls, mainly her late husband Albert and occasionally a Himalayan named Toto. On other occasions, a "master" named Hassan has also manifested through her. It would take an entire book to list the exploits of this incredible medium, and space will not permit me to do so. As a matter of fact, Ethel Meyers has been at work on her autobiography for some time now and it will be published before long.

In a personal sitting, February 17, 1971, Ethel spoke of the birth of our second baby. "When will the baby be born?" I asked. "March to April. Could be the 4th or 5th." Our second daughter was born April 5th. I mention this because the majority of mediums, even the best ones, are generally unable to pinpoint dates very accurately. While predictions may be extremely correct in detail, the timing may be way off. This has to do with the fact that in a timeless dimension there simply isn't any way to read a date. But Ethel Meyers does on occasion get exact dates.

As her own horizons expanded, so did the nature of her readings. It is an undeniable fact that part of a psychic reading is from the other side, if the medium has this particular talent, part from the medium's own unconscious, and best described as ESP ability, but part also the digested knowledge acquired by the medium as a human being, through reading, through learning, and through discussions with others. As Ethel Meyers became more and more interested in reincarnation, she began to give people readings concerning their past lives. It is no more possible to prove that these readings are accurate than it is to prove that they are not. Such impressions of past lives and the connections be-

tween the individuals in this life belong in the realms of metaphysics, of course, and have nothing to do with evidential
material. But I am convinced that Mrs. Meyers gives these
readings from a source other than herself, awakened somehow
by her own interest in the subject.

Another area that has fascinated this medium for some
time is the gift of psychic photography. Mrs. Meyers has experimented with photographic paper, producing what is generally known as *scotographs*. The light sensitive paper is held
to the stomach area, the solar plexus, then it is exposed to an
electric light for a few moments and developed in regular
developing fluid. The result shows various forms, some of
them looking like faces and human beings. Unfortunately, the
very fact that the paper is exposed to electric light under un-
controlled conditions takes the evidential value out of the
experiment. But it is interesting that faces that have been
recognized as those of deceased relatives, have appeared on
these experimental scotographs whether or not they were obtained under scientific conditions.

Those who wish to consult Mrs. Meyers professionally fall
into three categories. They are, first of all, those who need
personal counsel and hope to obtain it through a combination
of pastoral advice based upon intuitive processes and communication with a dead relative, presumed to be ahead in
knowledge and therefore useful to the seeker; there are those
who are fascinated by the possibility of contact with another
world, researchers or amateurs, who find the possibility of
such contact exciting and stimulating; and there are those
who seek the medium's help in specific projects, whether research projects or treasure hunts or the quest for a missing
person, or perhaps the solution to a crime. Ethel Meyers attempts to help all of these people in her own way. At times, she
takes the roundabout path to give them what they want, because as a Scorpio Ethel Meyers is not a woman of a few
words. Some of her work comes from herself, consciously and

directly. Much of it, especially when she is in trance or even in a borderline state of semitrance, is inspired by what she is told either by her guide, Albert, or some other spirit entity. There is no doubt in my mind that Mrs. Meyers is at times controlled by other individuals; her facial muscles rearrange themselves, her expression, her voice, her movements, and of course her storehouse of personal knowledge are those of others than herself. No actress in the world could impersonate these other individuals with such accuracy, with such intimate knowledge of their lives. During one of my early investigations with Mrs. Meyers as a medium, it was suggested by a "modern scientist" that the results, her intimate knowledge of Civil War engagements, were due to her ability to send part of her mind to the New York Public Library and raid the respective files for information, then return to the rest of herself and furnish me with the desired material. Sometimes the proffered explanations from materialistically oriented scientists are far more unbelievable than the most outrageous claims anyone in the psychic field could put forth.

Mrs. Meyers accepts applications in writing and notifies the prospective clients of her availability. Her fees are between twenty-five and fifty dollars but depend on individual services and circumstances. She also does group sittings and sees clients in their own homes as well as at her studio. However, she prefers for them to come to her New York studio. Mrs. Meyers does not visit haunted houses on her own because she realizes the dangers of doing such work without the help of a parapsychologist. On occasion, she will help a possessed person, when she feels she can do so safely. It must be understood that Ethel Meyers is a well-read and knowledgeable individual, far more than just a channel of communication, and that at times she is a capable counselor in the field of the occult as well as a good medium. Mrs. Ethel Johnson Meyers may be reached at: 160 West Seventy-third Street, New York, New York 10023. **Recommended.**

John Reeves is a school teacher who took to mediumship at first to supplement his income, later as a main occupation, and still later, after returning to teaching, again as a part-time occupation. He was originally brought to my attention by the late Betty Ritter under whom he had studied. Looking like a southern school teacher, which after all he was, and not at all like a psychic, Mr. Reeves gave me a number of private sessions, all of them highly interesting and evidential. His psychic ability had started at age twelve and he began to see headlines before the newspapers printed them. "In 1961, I saw a headline involving Superintendent Theobald, and I knew it was going to be a bit scandalous. I picked up the newspaper in the morning, not finding it in the headline; however, that afternoon I saw a later edition and it was in that." The South Carolina-born Reeves also predicted that a new pyramid would be discovered southwest of Cairo. Not much later, a pyramid was actually discovered. Mr. Reeves has a B.A. with a major in literature and served in the U.S. Navy prior to his arrival in New York. He is primarily a clairvoyant, seeing events before they occur. I have published some of his exploits in an earlier book, *The Prophets Speak*. Mr. John Reeves's last known address was: 225 East Seventy-fourth Street, New York, New York 10021. **Recommended.**

Virginia Cloud has vigorously defended her position as an amateur medium for all the years I've known her, yet her ability ranks with any professional, sometimes with amazing results. Miss Cloud is essentially a librarian, researcher, and writer, from a southern background, and extremely well connected in two areas—motion picture history and southern society. I have written of her predictions in *The Prophets Speak* and have also reported on some of her psychic encounters with ghosts. Virginia uses tarot cards to induce psychic impressions. Frequently, however, she gets flashes and then calls me on the telephone to ask me whether such and such makes any sense to me. Much of what she has told me over the years has later come true. On June 16, 1968, she asked me whether the names "Hardwick" and "Crewe" made any sense to me. Both of these are not exactly common names. It so happened that I met a young woman named Hardwick, whose case I investigated in the Philadelphia area, a most unusual case of a "time slip." As for Crewe, it was fully a year later that I visited and investigated the Lord Crewe Arms Hotel in England. Long before the death of Aristotle Onassis' son, Virginia felt that tragedy would befall that family. On January 2, 1972, Virginia said she saw "a separation from one of our children. Perhaps Nadine will go away, maybe to school, which will indeed be to her advantage." We did not decide on this move until the spring of 1974. On June 9, 1971, Virginia Cloud also proved to me that she has contact with "the other world." In a reading given to me at that time, she mentioned three individuals who were calling on her, Henry, Alice, and Julius. All three are close relatives of mine, all three are deceased, and at no time did I discuss them with Virginia. Those wishing Virginia Cloud to do a reading for them, whether in person, or in her strange way by consulting her cards, may contact her at: Post Office Box 2684, Grand Central Station, New York, New York 10017. The charge is twenty-five dollars per reading. **Recommended.**

Carol White is a young woman who specializes in crystal ball reading, more technically called scrying. She also does tarot reading and has done spontaneous psychic impressions in my class at the New York Institute of Technology with good results. At times she can get impressions from touching a client's palm, or even on the way to see a client, psychic information will come to her unsought. This includes data concerning the person's health. Carol White may be reached by writing: 103 West Eightieth Street, New York, New York 10024. Telephone: 212-868-4028. **Satisfactory.**

Shawn Robbins is a young woman in her late twenties, whom I have known and worked with since 1969. At that time, she appeared in various nightclubs as a psychic reader, while simultaneously pursuing a career in music, both writing and playing. At various times she has held down office jobs as well, although her first love is the psychic world. Her early experiences include veridical dreams, encounters with the spirit of her grandmother, warnings, and especially information concerning future events, headlines, airplane accidents, and such. For a while she was on the payroll of a major industrial concern, giving predictions concerning the stock market. I have also tested Shawn in a number of haunted houses, taking her to locations she knew nothing about. In each case she came up with evidential information, and though she is not a trance medium, her clairvoyance is detailed and significant. Recently, she has added the art of astrology to her interests, and her readings frequently take on astrological overtones. This may be due to a long and fruitful association with astrologer Gar Osten, now a resident of Iowa, with whom she worked closely. For several years, I subjected Shawn to brief treatments with electromagnetism, using the experimental machine developed by Dr. Douglas Baker of England with excellent results. Not only did some minor physical problems Shawn was suffering from clear up considerably, but her psychic perception also increased one hundred percent. Apparently, placing her head into a low level magnetic field for fifteen to twenty minutes at a time somehow encouraged her psychic ability to the point at which she was stronger and more evidential in her work. Shawn Robbins's predictions that have come true are many, and some are quite spectacular. At times, her honesty may be shocking to those for whom the prediction is made, but in a way, such honesty serves as an early warning and allows the recipient of bad news to be prepared for it. Such was the case when she told a friend that the baby he and his wife were expecting would be lost. It turned out that the unfortunate prediction was correct. On September 20, 1970, Shawn asked me whether the name "Kaufman" meant anything to me. It didn't then, but in early 1974, the Kaufman case was one of the most interesting cases of possession I have ever been involved in. Shawn Robbins gives private readings to individuals and also works with businesses requiring commercial counsel. She lectures to groups and gives demonstrations, and also does astrological charts, interpreting them, however, from the psychic point of view. Although she has made somewhat of a speciality of predicting airplane crashes, she is by no means a prophetess of doom. Those wishing to contact her may do so by calling 212-TW6-1892 in Queens, New York. **Recommended.**

Richard Madden is one of the newer young mediums starting a career in the New York area. At age six, he sensed the presence of a spirit around himself, not knowing at the time what it meant. He saw shadowy forms that would come and go; he was special even as a child. When Madden was nineteen years old, he first heard voices of people he could not see. He could not identify the voices, however. Madden is a native of Florida, his father is a military career man, currently working for an airline. He is one of seven children, and currently has a day job in a day care center for children. Three years ago, he began giving readings to friends, using tarot cards as inducing agents. "It is something from within," he explained to me. "There is something in my head saying this and that." Mr. Madden was brought to my attention by Elaine Sturtevant, self-styled psychic scout, who has also been responsible for my acquaintanceship with the Australian clairvoyant, John Gaudry. Those wishing to try Mr. Madden may reach him at 212-861-4197. **Satisfactory.**

Maria Bleiker is a spunky lady of eighty three, living in Yorkville with a pudgy little dog whom she adores. German-born, she has been a professional opera singer for many years, always cognizant of her ability with the tarot cards and astrology. Eventually, she became a professional in this field. The appearance and trappings of Mrs. Bleiker are simple and almost in the vein of the tea leaf reader. But this appearance is deceiving, because Mrs. Bleiker does not dispense generalities. She is a genuine psychic, has a good grasp of astrology as well, and works diligently and sincerely at her craft. I have consulted her four or five times since 1970, and to this day she does not know who I am, or even remembers my name correctly; consequently, she cannot be accused of having foreknowledge about me from my books or television appearances. Nevertheless, she was extremely evidential with me from the very first reading onward. The only question she asks of the client is the birthdate, because she does combine astrological interpretation with her psychic readings. With her card reading, she does the lengthy method of shuffling and dealing, shuffling and dealing again and so forth, until every "house" of the person being read has been investigated. This may take as much as forty-five minutes. Mrs. Bleiker works mainly with average people, sincere seekers, not necessarily psychic researchers. For those wishing to consult her, her dog's name is Mitzi. Mrs. Bleiker grew up near Coblentz. Her parents both drowned when she was nine months old. Some of the material she brings through seems to be of a Spiritualist nature because it involves information on discarnate people. The fee for her card reading is eight dollars. Her astrological chart costs fourteen dollars. Mrs. Bleiker may be contacted at: 337 East Eighty-sixth Street, New York, New York 10028. Telephone: 212-SA2-6236. **Satisfactory.**

Barry and Jackie Shawney are a young couple working together as a psychic team. Mrs. Shawney is able to give readings from a photograph, while Mr. Shawney is clairvoyant. The Shawneys are just beginning to become professional, giving private readings by previous arrangement. Mr.

and Mrs. Shawney may be reached at: 470 Fifty-fourth Street, Brooklyn, New York 11220. **No comment.**

A somewhat unusual psychic is Frederick Stoessel. In his middle forties and a college graduate, Stoessel was a combat naval officer and has headed his own business management firm for a number of years. He is a well-known financial consultant and business adviser. Some years ago, Stoessel withdrew from organized religion and became involved with Christian Science. Gradually his own ESP powers fascinated him even more until he decided to develop them and use them. Few psychics can foretell their own future, but Stoessel is an exception. While still a student at New York University, he had a recurrent dream in which he saw Oriental soldiers swarming over a certain hill. He discussed it with his mother, because the dream disturbed him greatly. In June of that same year, North Korea attacked South Korea, and suddenly the dream stopped. A few days later he was called into the navy and sent to Korea.

Stoessel's main interests were in finance and politics, and he has been amazingly accurate in calling the shots in both. Eventually he began to publish a privately circulated newsletter in which he made predictions of possible future events in both areas. At first, he couched his language in cautious terms, using the term *psychic* rarely if at all. Lately, he has discovered his ability to heal people and has added psychic healing to his activities. "For healing, an initial letter is required outlining the nature of the problem and details as to a regular doctor's treatment. Religious background would also be appreciated." Stoessel corresponds with the patient via tape cassette, and no charges are made for the service, although donations to cover cassette and mailing are accepted. Stoessel does not claim to be a medical doctor and always advises potential clients to seek competent medical advice first. Only when the latter fails, does he wish to be involved. In

1971, he discontinued his company of financial and loan brokers, and devoted himself exclusively to his occult work.

Mr. Stoessel believes he can help anyone solve their problems, whether emotional, medical, or financial by helping people discover their own solutions and inner strength. In this respect, his work seems to be largely metaphysical. "A woman who was undergoing a divorce called me stating that she was being awakened in the night with severe flu and head conditions. I realized that it was the rage of the husband being sent to her mentally. I declared that only God and the qualities of God controlled him. They subsided at once," Mr. Stoessel declares. Frederick Stoessel also lectures to groups on the various areas of psychic phenomena in which he is involved. Those wishing to get his newsletter or bring their problems to him, may write to him at: Box 5012 Woolsey Station, Long Island City, New York 11105. Telephone: 212-545-9223. **Recommended.**

Phyllis Woodbury is a psychic reader coming into prominence in recent months. By coincidence, if there be such a thing, she makes her headquarters at the very same place where the late Carolyn Chapman first worked. Miss Woodbury is a sincere, dedicated psychic who gives private readings by appointment. She may be found at the Hotel Ansonia, Broadway at Seventy-third Street, or reached by telephone at 212-874-6393 in New York City. **No comment.**

Those who want their psychics on an elevated plane, away from the mundane details of financial or business success, and who seek the greater spiritual truth in their lives rather than a glimpse of their own future, may find Alfreda Oliver just their cup of tea. This lively English lady has her own church, a small but tenacious following, and is also available for private readings. Mrs. Oliver came to California under the prodding of her spiritual guide, and for a number of years she conducted her Spiritualist church services in Los Angeles.

Eventually she removed to New York and again formed various groups to whom she teaches her particular brand of metaphysics. Her specialty, in her own words, is auric readings, and her teachings are based upon the influence of the aura on human consciousness and health. Although Mrs. Oliver has had a number of routine psychic experiences herself, and freely acknowledges the existence of spirit communication, she is not particularly engaged in message work or psychic reading in the ordinary sense. Her study groups are quite small, but she likes to work with individuals to a great extent. Basically, Mrs. Oliver is a metaphysical teacher, with methods representing a blend of Oriental and Western thinking. She herself is a picture of health, far younger looking than her years, and very definitely an enjoyable person. Address: 160 West Seventy-third Street, New York, New York 10023. Her telephone is listed under Sherman Square Studios in New York City. **Satisfactory.**

Gene Sullivan's main profession is in art as a painter. She has a number of one-woman shows to her credit and is well known in art circles. Her psychic talent is strictly a secondary pursuit, but she does it so well that it may yet become a major activity for her. Miss Sullivan's particular phase of mediumship is palmistry, the reading of character and future in the lines of the hands. Gene Sullivan makes prints of her client's hands, keeps them on file, and compares them with developments from time to time. By comparing the change in the hand lines and weighing them against actual events in a person's life, she is able to foretell future developments in that person's life. It is comparatively little known that the lines in a person's hands do change over the years, so that a reading foretelling the destiny of an individual is correct only at that moment. Either free will or circumstances thrust upon the individual may change the course of events, which then will reflect themselves in the altered nature of the lines in the hand. By keeping track with prints of the hands, Gene

Sullivan has put the art of palmistry on a quasi-scientific level, apart from the fact that her interpretations are extremely detailed and accurate. She freely admits that she combines a visual interpretation of the hand lines she has studied with psychic intuition. In this way her readings go far beyond those of many professional palmists, such as those of popular nightclubs, who simply look at the hand lines and interpret them according to the books they have read. It is not altogether amazing that the hand lines should disclose future trends in a person's life or clues to that person's behavior. It is no more amazing than the fact that healers can diagnose illness from the appearance and condition of the iris of the eye, which they can. Personality is a whole, and one part of it reflects in all the other parts. Gene Sullivan may be reached in New York City at 212-CI5-0347. **Recommended.**

Those who are interested in numerology as a means of divining the future, or getting to know their own nature better, will find Ariel Yvon Taylor an interesting reader. Mrs. Taylor, advanced in years and knowledge, uses numbers to determine a person's basic characteristics, outlook, and future trends. In a way, numerology relates to astrology in that it gives indications of trends rather than actual events to take place. If everything in the universe can eventually be reduced to mathematical equations, as some scientists think, then the numerical value of names, whether at birth or assumed, has some significance. It is the contention of numerologists like Mrs. Taylor that the right combination of numerals in a person's name can lead to success, while the wrong name, as represented by the wrong configuration of numbers, may hold a person back. She computes complicated charts from the name and birth data of her clients, and explains the various aspects of her client's name in relation to professional activities, love and success, and other attributes of personality. Ariel Yvon Taylor maintains a studio at Carnegie Hall, Fifty-seventh

Street and Seventh Avenue, New York, New York. **Recommended.**

Lynn Vaan Cleef is a young astrologer making his home in New York City. A school teacher by education and profession, Mr. Vaan Cleef turned professional astrologer in 1973 as a result of a deepening interest in the occult sciences. He describes himself as a "spiritual astrologer," the first and only time I have heard this term, and has taught his craft at the University of Michigan, Ann Arbor. "The seriousness of his commitment and his qualifications as an astrologer and student of the occult are unquestionable," says Marilyn Shaw, Educational Director of that University. Mr. Vaan Cleef also teaches classes and gives psychic and tarot readings, as well as hand analysis. Those wishing to test his skills may reach him at: #1 Sherman Square, New York, New York 10023. Telephone: 212-873-2698. **No Comment.**

Charles Jayne is one of the most brilliant technical astrologers in the field, concentrating mainly on research these days. He is associated with the Astro-Psychological Consultation Center, a school of astrology with several qualified teachers in residence. Mr. Jayne has taken part in a number of investigations in years past, during which medium Ethel Johnson Meyers was able to bring allegedly deceased astrologers "through" for the purpose of being interrogated on highly technical matters by Mr. Jayne, with good results. Sharing quarters with this specialized service is the more generally oriented Astrological Bureau, founded in 1953. A staff of resident astrologers provides classes and lectures in the field as well as private consultations. Those wishing to contact them can do so at: 111 East Sixty-first Street, New York, New York 10012. Telephone: 212-371-5282. **Recommended.**

Zoltan Mason is not only the owner of a highly specialized bookshop in the field of astrology, but he is also an astrology teacher who gives a number of private consultations by appointment. Mr. Mason knows his craft well, frequently differs in opinion or interpretation with his colleagues, and is somewhat of a colorful personality in the field. Those wishing to contact him may find him at: 789 Lexington Avenue, New York, New York. Telephone: 212-832-8958. **Satisfactory.**

Isidor Oblo, also a colorful citizen, has been a recognized astrologer for many years, always at the same address. Mr. Oblo has a faithful following and does not advertise. His charts, while undoubtedly the result of sound astrological training, nevertheless show a degree of psychic intuition as well. Those wishing to book a session with him may find him at: 240 West End Avenue, New York, New York 10023. Telephone: 212-TR4-1322. **Recommended.**

The dean of astrologers is Hugh MacCraig, a man in his eighties who has had an interesting career as a motion picture actor. When an accident disfigured his face, he had to turn to other ways of making a living. Many years ago he discovered astrology, and in the course of some thirty years as a practicing astrologer, has become somewhat of a legend in his own time. I consulted Mr. MacCraig twenty-five years ago, at which time he predicted events in my life that are just coming to pass, and very accurately at that. Mr. MacCraig likes to take his time in casting a horoscope, requesting data about his prospective client prior to meeting the client. When he meets with his client, he has the chart drawn and can give a personal interpretation. Those wishing to consult this venerable and gifted astrologer may contact him at: 10 East Thirty-ninth Street, New York, New York 10016. Telephone: 212-532-0016. **Recommended.**

North Carolina

Sean Harribance has an unlikely first name for an Indian, but Mr. Harribance has a distinguished record of cooperation with Professor Joseph Rhine, who has praised him as one of the outstanding psychics of our time. The Trinidad-born Harribance, in his middle thirties, scores high on scientific tests and takes a self-critical attitude toward his own abilities. He travels around the country and gives lecture demonstrations in major population centers.

William Roll, another North Carolina researcher who has worked with the West Indian, is quoted by a national weekly newspaper as saying, "he does many things extremely well. Most psychics perform well in one field and fail in others. But Sean can be tested in mind over matter and clairvoyance experiments as well as in other ESP experiments."

Those wishing to contact this psychic, may find him in Durham, North Carolina, where he also holds down a department store job. Undoubtedly, he can be contacted through Dr. Joseph B. Rhine or William Roll at the Psychical Research Foundation, Duke Station, Durham, North Carolina 27706. **Satisfactory.**

Ohio

Komar the Hindu fakir is not a psychic but an extremely agile performer of well-known Hindu fakir tricks, showing superb mastery along yoga traditions. Those who are interested in the physical aspects of the occult may derive some benefit from contact with him. Komar, whose civilian name is Vernon Craig, also manufactures an excellent cheese. He may be reached at: 323 Ihrig Avenue, Wooster, Ohio 44691. **Satisfactory.**

There is an interesting old lady in Cincinnati, Ohio, who compares favorably with some of the British Spiritualist readers. Mrs. Burrows was brought to my attention by Virginia Cameron, the president of the Parapsychology Forum of that city, in 1970. Mrs. Burrows granted me a sitting, during which she brought some extremely evidential material to my attention. Among other things, she told me right off the bat that my wife had a little girl on the way, at the time when Mrs. Burrows neither knew that I was married nor that my wife was pregnant. The medium further stated that my wife needed a buildup and had a low blood count. My wife is anemic. Mrs. Burrows does not see too many people because of her advanced age. She can best be contacted through the Parapsychology Forum of Cincinnati: Post Office Box 24105, Cincinnati, Ohio 45224. Her fee is $10.00. **Recommended.**

Oregon

Penny Hale claims to be ninety-five percent (95%) accurate in her prophecies and predictions. Her claims to fame include exact predictions of the current energy and water shortages, of the Washington government scandal, and of other public events. Miss Hale, who operates under the name of Psychic Research Association, although she is not an association, may be contacted for possible private sittings at: Post Office Box 125, Beaverton, Oregon 97005. **No comment.**

Pennsylvania

Mrs. Marianne Elko has figured in several of my books as a particularly gifted psychic capable of getting visions of future events, especially those pertaining to world politics. She has given me ample proof of her ability to receive communications from discarnates by providing me spontaneously with intimate details of the manner of their death and of their family situations. At that time, none of this information on these discarnates had been published, and Mrs. Elko did not have access to information concerning my private affairs. Among the amazing things she told me in a sitting three years ago, was the statement that my brother-in-law was present in spirit and wished to converse with me. "He says he died on the twenty-third of December," Mrs. Elko stated. "He wanted to live at least to the twenty-sixth because he thought he would ruin your Christmas, but he couldn't, it was a car accident. He always comes through before the twenty-ninth of September, your wedding anniversary." None of these very precise data could have been known to Mrs. Elko at the time she made the statement.

Mrs. Elko is a school teacher by vocation. For a while, her psychic interests brought her into conflict with her superiors, but they have long since accepted her unusual talent, especially as she was able to prove to their satisfaction that her readings had prevented some serious calamities at times and have brought the school board no adverse publicity. Marianne Elko, who was born in Germany, may be reached at: 2207 Riverview Drive, Industry, Pennsylvania 15052. **Recommended.**

5

How to Consult
an Occult Practitioner

The first step in learning about the various forms of psychic activities is to consult directories, such as this, or listen to word of mouth, which in this field is particularly significant. But finding the appropriate person to consult is only half the job. If the reader is to derive full benefit from such an association, he or she should know how to behave, what to do and what not to do, and how to evaluate the result of such encounters. One of the greatest problems in this field is not the large number of frauds operating in it, because that number is very small; rather it is the uncritical attitude of the individuals consulting professionals in the occult field, coupled with a false expectation on the part of many, that makes it so difficult to speak of universally acceptable results.

To begin with, a medium or whatever psychic practitioner one consults is only an intermediary between some information or a personality, allegedly deceased, and the one seeking this information or person. The first thing to forget is that notion that the professional consultant is some sort of supernatural being, possessing powers that in themselves are capable of changing the world, performing seeming miracles, or otherwise behaving in contradiction to natural law. In earlier centuries, mediumship was frequently considered a gift of God, denied other human beings, and it gave the one who exercised it the aura of the supernatural. Sometimes this led to near religious worship of psychics; sometimes the very same psychics were accused of being in league with the devil. In the days of the Old Testament, prophets were considered extraordinary human beings somewhere between man and God, certainly not ordinary citizens. Christianity has tended to make mediumship either a saintly device, in which the mediumistic personality speaks as a vehicle of God, or a diabolical instrument, in which case the messages coming from the medium are to be considered evil. Christianity hasn't been able to place mediumistic individuals into a category of their own, to accept psychic phenomena as natural forms of human consciousness. Nearly every other religion has ascribed special attributes to people capable of functioning as psychics, ranging all the way from inspiration to divinity. Sometimes the mediumistic individual is referred to simply as a master, at other times the medium is possessed by the deity itself, but the notion that mediums could simply be people with a particularly high degree of sensitivity to vibrations carrying thought energies has not found acceptance in any religious establishment. It is only in the light of today's scientific understanding that mediums are properly classed as individuals with greater sensitivies than the average. We know that the dividing line between sensory perception and extrasensory perception is thin and flexible indeed, and that being mediumistic is by no means unnatural or "supernatural."

It is well to remember this and not to approach a sitting or public reading with a sense of awe, but rather with a healthy curiosity, and a balanced approach that allows neither for extreme skepticism nor for uncritical belief. Always remember that the person giving the psychic reading, or the astrologer or numerologist or whatever, is a professional performing a service as well as he or she can, that the practitioner may fail at times and succeed at others, that he or she may be good with one person and not good with another, and that, in sum total, you are dealing with a fellow human being not so much different from yourself.

Everybody is born with the gift of ESP; it is potentially inherent in man. With some people it develops to a larger degree than with others, in some cases it is encouraged through tolerance and interest, in others it is ignored or suppressed. But the fact remains that ESP is not a mysterious sixth sense, as some would have it, but merely the extension of the ordinary five senses as we know them beyond the limits we have been brought up to believe were their boundaries, but that in fact are not. ESP, psychic ability, is therefore a natural function of all our senses, and it is the absence of this faculty that makes us "subnormal," not the presence of it that makes us "supernatural." Primitive societies have maintained a larger degree of this ability, and to this day the natives of some remote areas use telepathy to communicate with each other the way we use the telephone. Partly through a materialistically oriented industrialized society, and partly through social and religious prejudices, sophisticated modern man has lost to a large extent the natural ability of ESP. This is not to say that he cannot regain it by enlarging his environment to take in many aspects he has deliberately ignored in the past. Those who have prevailed over such restrictive conditions and have maintained a considerable degree of psychic ability despite it discover somewhere along the line that they have unusual gifts, and some of them turn these gifts into a profession. This is no different than, let us say, a musically inclined person discovering a talent for the piano. It is a talent that can either remain a hobby for the amusement of one's family, or if pursued, become a professional way of life, a way to earn a living as a concert pianist or popular piano player. The choice is potentially everyone's, depending only upon environmental pressure, personality factors, individual likes and dislikes, or potential acceptance by the public of one's professional activities.

If you have chosen a particular practitioner to consult, make sure you do not give more than your name, and not necessarily your real name. I have often tested mediums by giving a fictitious name, only to find that the really good ones will get my actual name in the course of the sitting. I recall the late Lillian Bailey of London, of whom I had heard a great deal. In order to make sure that the test would be adequate, I refrained from communicating with her directly, but asked the editor of the *Psychic News* to make the arrangements for me. Mr. Maurice Barbanell, the editor, thereupon called Lillian Bailey in my presence, asking her to arrange for a sitting with a certain Mr. Wood, for whom he could vouch. This was necessary as mediums are sometimes harrassed by newspaper reporters disguising themselves as believers, or even an occasional policeman trying to stir up trouble.

After I had arrived in the suburban home of Lillian Bailey and had taken a seat opposite her, she went into deep trance, and her control, a Scottish doctor, took over her speech mechanism. Within a matter of three or four minutes, this control exclaimed: "Why, you are not Mr. Wood at all. Your name is Hans Holzer." Needless to say, I was surprised. A hostile reporter would assume that the editor of the *Psychic News* had informed Miss Bailey of my true name, but such was not the case, because Mr. Barbanell is as scrupulous in his work as he is reliable in his integrity.

Nothing would be lost if you were to give a false name, if that is your desire. On the other hand, if your name is of little meaning to a stranger, there is no need to do so. In my case, disclosure of my real name would automatically disqualify any material concerning my published career. In the case of an ordinary or average individual, little is likely to be known to the medium consciously, and if in making the appointment no address is given, even the remote possibility of a dishonest medium's checking up on a prospective sitter would be eliminated. In all the years I have tested mediums, I have never met a medium who went to the trouble of checking up on a sitter's personal circumstances. It is true that Spiritualists maintain cards concerning regular visitors to their camps and that these cards are frequently passed from one medium to another in a fraudulent manner. But the material on these cards is obtained in routine sittings, and no one goes out of his way to collect a file on individual sitters for the sole purpose of defrauding them.

Very few psychics can do a full reading without sitting opposite the client, especially the first time. On occasion, I have been given bits of information of a psychic nature on the telephone by such renowned mediums as the late Betty Ritter or by Ethel Johnson Meyers, but that I think is due to the fact that we have sat together many times and that a permanent link had thus been established beforehand. On first acquaintance, a personal visit is always recommended. People who would like to take the easy route of obtaining psychic readings by mail (or telephone) are only deceiving themselves. Those who dispense such reading without prior personal contact are either extraordinarily gifted mediums or unusually cynical.

Once an appointment has been made, it should be kept, and kept on time. Reputable psychics apportion their time very carefully because they can do just so many readings a day. Otherwise, they might endanger their health, and if not that, at least their accuracy. Psychic work requires physical energy, and that energy must be replenished through rest and sleep in order to be readily available at full strength. Some mediums can do as many as ten to fifteen readings a day, half an hour each, only to fall exhausted at the end of the day. Others take but a single client a day. It is difficult to set norms for such work, as every medium knows his or her own strength. Probably the safest number of readings per day lies somewhere between two and six. Whether you are going to the residence of the psychic reader or expect the reader to come to yours, the etiquette is the same. One should be as relaxed as possible, ask permission if a tape recorder is to be used, and should not smoke, unless encouraged to do so by the medium. Incredibly, some mediums do smoke and rather heavily, although it is essentially not conducive to their work. But then one of the best and most evidential psychic healers preceded his work with extreme sexual activities, which he believed supplied him with the necessary "fuel" to perform his work.

It is not only all right but useful to exchange a few generalities with the psychic reader, especially if it is the first time that you have met him or her. This relaxes both parties and sets up a vibrational bridge between reader and client. The voice serves as a link, regardless of what is being said. Naturally, the conversation should not contain leading material that would be brought up during the actual sitting. You should never tell the reader why you are seeing her or him, only ask for a sitting. It is a common and unfortunate mistake to book a psychic for consultation and then to go into the reasons for the consultation. It is understandable, especially if the reasons are compelling ones or emotionally motivated, but in doing so, the client removes a large element of believability from the resulting material. The ideal appointment is made by name only, and no information about the nature of the business, the reason for the sitting, or anything else concerning the sitter is divulged to the psychic. The initial conversation, which should not last beyond three or four minutes, can concern itself with the weather, with the difficulties or lack of same in reaching the place for the sitting, or it can touch on psychic research in general, books one has read, and so on. Personal business should be kept out of the conversation. By the same token, beware of the psychic who asks personal questions right off the bat. A reputable medium will not ask questions, she or he will make statements that the sitter can either accept or deny. Among Spiritualist mediums there have been a number of those who thrived on seemingly innocent questions that supplied them with the bulk of their "psychic information." Such deceit was possible only with the collaboration of the naive sitter, of course. A sitter who does not answer leading questions is not likely to be deceived.

On the other hand, once the sitting begins, and most psychic readers or mediums will give their clients a sign that they are getting "into" the sitting, full attention should be paid to everything that is coming from the lips of the psychic. If the reader is merely a clairvoyant, using personal psychic abilities to give the reading, information will be coming forth almost immediately. If the psychic is of the Spiritualist persuasion, there may be alleged communications from spirits supplying the medium with information he or she gives to the sitter. In the case of trance mediums, a control will first speak through the entranced medium, announcing himself or herself, and frequently this will be followed by discarnates speaking directly with the sitter through the medium. In the latter case, it is permissible for the sitter to reply. When the psychic practitioner speaks as herself or himself, giving information obtained through ESP, the sitter need only take notice. At times, the medium may ask confirmation or denial of a statement made. If that is the case, it is quite sufficient to say, yes, no, or maybe. Any elaboration beyond that while the sitting is still in progress is self-defeating. On the other hand, once the sitting has been concluded, the sitter should feel free to comment upon the accuracy or lack of same displayed by the medium. But even then it should be kept in mind that the sitter might wish to return for another session at some future date. Consequently, the information disclosed by the psychic practitioner at this first meeting and confirmed by the sitter might become a repetitive element the next time, in which case it no longer has any evidential value whatsoever. Therefore, when additional sittings are contemplated by a client, extreme paucity of words and cautious confirmation should be employed, sufficient to reassure the medium that he or she has done a good job but not sufficiently elaborate to furnish the medium with information that he or she could use consciously or unconsciously in future sittings. This does not mean that the medium may do this fraudulently, but that the medium's unconscious mind may pick up information in this manner that will reappear on future occasions.

At times, a psychic may be unable to make the necessary contact, perhaps because a sitter is too "cold," that is, has put up a defensive shield knowingly or unknowingly, or because of personal circumstances concerning the medium. In order not to disappoint the sitter, an object will be requested that will become an inducing agent for the medium to get "into" the vibration of the sitter. Through psychometry, the ball gets rolling, so to speak, and the reading proceeds. There are of course mediums who are strictly psychometrists, who can do nothing but interpret impressions gained from touching an object belonging to a certain person.

Psychic practitioners run the gamut from excellent and evidential to bad, just as human beings differ greatly in their personalities. A client has a right to demand a certain level of performance if a professional is being paid for a sitting. A client should not be satisfied with generalities, well-meaning pastoral advice, and statements about alleged dead relatives so vague that they could fit anyone. In particular, names or at least initials of individuals referred to by the medium should be demanded, specific circumstances and detailed descriptions of events alluded to should be requested, and in general a channeling of the medium's abilities toward a reasonably accurate description of events or persons should be expected. The late Eileen Garrett, probably one of the world's greatest mediums, was extremely adamant about poor performance by "sloppy" mediums. She always insisted that a medium come up with dates and names, detailed circumstances, and evidential material each time out. Her own training by the late Dr. Hewitt Mackenzie of the British College of Psychic Studies had made her into the great and evidential medium she became, and she wanted no less from her colleagues in the field.

The uninitiated sitter sometimes has strange ideas as to fees for psychic work. Some individuals even consider payment for unsuccessful sittings not called for, making the work strictly speculative in their minds. I recall how the late motion picture actress Miriam Hopkins asked the late Betty Ritter to come to her house for a reading. Miss Hopkins was herself highly psychic, and also very difficult to get along with at times. I do not know what happened between the two ladies, but apparently Miss Hopkins was not altogether satisfied with the reading given her by the medium. She refused to pay her. When I discovered this, I took into account the work put in by Betty Ritter and the financial status of the late movie star and asked her to pay Betty Ritter for her time, whether she liked the reading or not. In some states, for reasons of law, psychic practitioners do not charge for their work per se, but for the time given to a client. After all, a medical doctor does not charge for successful healing, but only for the effort and his time and knowledge. If the doctor fails, the patient doesn't get his money back.

What then is a proper fee? There are those who prefer to go to a public sitting, whether in a Spiritualist church or some other accessible place, a meeting where anywhere from five to fifty people are in the audience, being read individually and publicly. Sometimes, especially with well-known mediums, as many as one thousand fill major concert halls for the sole purpose of receiving messages from their beloved ones on the other side of life. In these cases, a modest contribution of between two and five dollars is standard nowadays, and though it is called a "free will offering," it is really the expected thing to do. Private bookings run anywhere from five dollars to five hundred dollars, depending upon the medium. Most reputable mediums who have been established because of their evidential performance will charge between twenty and fifty dollars for a sitting, but there are some who will charge more, and there are many little known mediums of good quality who will give sittings for as little as five dollars.

What is considered good evidence and what is not? When a psychic reader whom you have just met for the first time tells you some pertinent facts about your own past or present, including names, dates, and situations, and if the majority of such statements are accurate, then it stands to reason that statements made about your future may also turn out to be accurate. Predictions concerning well-known people or those in the limelight of public attention cannot be taken seriously unless they are very specific. The fact that Mao Tse-tung may die within the following year is not a psychic prediction but a good guess, considering the man's age. The prediction that someone may try to shoot the president of the United States isn't psychic either; a president is a very likely target for a potential assassin, especially in times of stress. On the other hand, predictions concerning private individuals, who are not in the public eye, are more likely to be evidential, especially if they are precise and contain names and dates. I have quoted some of these amazing predictions with individual practitioners listed in this book. Evidence then consists of a fair percentage of hits, detailed material come true, and the absence of intensive questioning on the part of the medium. Do not expect a professional psychic to be good each time out, or to be equally as good with your friend as with you. A number of factors enter each reading, and conditions may vary the results a great deal. Mediums, on the other hand, should know better than to give sittings when they are physically low or emotionally disturbed.

You have only to open the pages of some popular magazines devoted to psychic phenomena and the occult in general to see the great range of practitioners available to the public. The advertising matter appearing in such magazines as *Fate* shows how many kinds of individuals vie for the consumer's dollar in this field. There are the legitimate ads from AMORC, the Rosicrucians of San Jose, California, there is the tightly written ad of the Universe Book Club, a Doubleday subsidiary, and there are the ads for the "Galaxy Gazer," a game produced for the Venture Book Shop, a subsidiary of the magazine itself. On the other hand, there are such pearls as this one: "Are you occult? Would you like to find out? For free lesson send postcard to ...." Or: "Are you unlucky? The girl whose dreams never come true? The man success passes by? Now you can do something about it! This age old symbol of Irish luck, the lucky leprechaun, cast in the original good luck mold from gleaming solid silver or gold can now be yours." How can you resist an ad reading, "You can use spiritual power and gain money," or "I dare you to be great. Do you want money, love, happiness, peace and success in special goals?" All you have to do is buy a certain book. "Now, right at home you can learn how to become a witch!" (Yes! I want to be a genuine witch. Send me lesson one of "You can become a witch," for which I enclose $4.95.) I especially liked this one: "Master your life. Call on secret guardians. Send $3.00, the month, day, year and hour of your birth, our researchers will send you the name of your own guardians, their powers and the ancient Solomonic rite known by the Old Ones." Or this one: "Giant power prayer. Send $5.00 for magic power prayer and blessed lucky numbers. Act now. Be surprised!"

Then there are those who advertise three questions for two or three dollars, by mail of course, and the self-appointed bishops of one-man or one-woman churches, the mysterious orders of this and that which exist only in the fertile imagination of the advertiser. Not all of these appear in *Fate* magazine, to be sure, but wherever these people look for clientele, beware of them.

If your quest is not for a psychic reading but for something beyond that, such as a so-called life reading, you should realize that there was only one Edgar Cayce, and as yet no one has come forward to equal his feats. So-called life readings offered by a number of well-meaning and some not so well-meaning individuals, at fees ranging from twenty to one hundred dollars, contain largely fantasies that cannot be checked out for veracity. Anyone with genuine memories of a previous life will come to realize his previous existence sooner or later through flashes of memory, through recurrent dreams, or through some form of déjà vu. Deliberately seeking out one's former lives, just out of curiosity, invites delusion. Occasionally, reputable mediums may obtain flashes of information about a sitter involving previous lifetimes. Ethel Johnson Meyers, one of the most reputable mediums around, frequently tells a sitter what he did in an earlier lifetime, or why he is going through certain difficulties in this one. I don't doubt Ethel Johnson Meyers's sincerity, nor the source of her information, but it is always difficult to prove such statements in the accepted scientific sense, unless actual names, dates, and situations are revealed that can be checked out.

Don't ask a medium to get in touch with a dead relative, don't induce communications, because you will either fail or fall victim to fraud. If a discarnate wishes to communicate with you for good reasons, he or she will find a way to get through to you. Reasons include the need to demonstrate continued existence in another dimension, unfinished business on the earth plane, or a state of difficulty in your own life that the discarnate relative or friend wishes to help you with. The best way to hope for such a contact is to sit with a competent psychic and open yourself up to whatever or whoever might "come through." A psychic reading is not a telephone communication. You cannot dial the person to whom you wish to speak, you cannot make demands other than to be given a reading containing as much identification and evidential material as the medium is capable of giving.

Another common misconception concerns the ability of the so-called dead to instruct the living in matters of superior knowledge. While it is true that discarnate relatives frequently help those on the earth plane by guiding them, they do so without breaking any of the laws of nature, and are in fact only helping people help themselves. Then, too, it should be realized that humans passing into the next dimension after physical death do not automatically acquire some superior spiritual or other knowledge, but are simply people existing in a dimension in which thought is the only reality. They, too, must learn to live in the new dimension and acquire knowledge that was denied them in their earthly existence. To assume that the spirit person has vastly superior foreknowledge is to delude oneself; on occasion, discarnates are permitted to divulge bits and pieces of information that might prove helpful to the person on the earth plane, but this is always done in accordance with universal law and under the control of the spirit guide supervising the communication. We should realize that the so-called spiritual dimension is as much subject to strict laws and natural conditions as is the denser, physical atmosphere in which we presently exist.

A reputable psychic will give honest readings without editing anything, whether the message is good or bad. This even includes warnings of danger or imminent death, because such knowledge should not be held back if the medium is truly an intermediary and nothing more. However, giving negative messages should be done in a cautious and soothing way, always leaving the door open to the possibility of error or misinterpretation. In this manner, the dire warning becomes merely a bit of foreknowledge with which the sitter is being armed, rather than the unfailing sword of Damocles hanging overhead, about which he cannot do anything. Sitters should never ask a professional psychic whether they see such and such in their future, or what they think about such and such a person. By mentioning an event or a specific person, or some special characteristic of themselves, and expecting the psychic to render an opinion, they are in fact only looking for an emotional crutch. Such crutches are more properly found among ministers and psychologists, not mediums. On the other hand, if a sitter is anxious about a certain aspect of his life, he may put the question in general terms, without divulging any detail, hoping that the psychic reader will come up with something that fits the situation. If the psychic does, the sitter should take into account the possibility of some thought reading entering the result, meaning that the psychic may very well pick up the sitter's own thoughts and intermingle them with genuine psychic material. In any event, living one's life by relying upon the opinions and predictions of psychic individuals is a poor way of spending one's time. Ultimately, all decisions rest with us, opportunities being thrust at us by fate. We are free to act, free to accept, reject, or ignore conditions around us, and while we seek the professional services of psychic practitioners, we should not abdicate our decision-making powers to them under any circumstances. If the majority of psychic professionals were infallible, then sitters consulting a number of such practitioners should obtain parallel readings. But they do not, frequently the readings differ or contain totally opposite material. Then again, there are many instances on record in which the same information is obtained from a variety of psychic professionals. I myself have obtained proof of the veracity of a number of such statements from half a dozen professional psychics who know nothing of each other or of me. On the whole, however, personal conditions of both sitter and psychic at the time of the reading, interpretations, prejudices, and other as yet not fully understood elements enter a reading, and results will never be one hundred percent identical, even if the same sitter consults a variety of readers. Ultimately, psychic readings help you to understand yourself better, give you an occasional glimpse of what lies ahead, and above all afford you the chance to be prepared for it when it comes. Readings of this kind also reassure your conviction that life goes on beyond physical death and that those who have gone before you are indeed alive and well and able to communicate with you at certain times and under certain conditions. The world of psychic professionals then complements the world of the living in such a way that it balances it, not replaces it, and the truly happy individual is one who lives his own life in a state of harmony, drawing on both sensory perceptions of the material world and extra-sensory knowledge from the next state of existence.

6

How to Be Your Own Medium

Despite the imposing number of psychic practitioners in both the major and minor cities in this country, there are wide areas where no such individuals reside and where the "service" of psychic readers, mediums, Spiritualist ministers, astrologers, numerologists, etc., is unavailable to people living in the area. Some are able to travel to the large cities where most psychics are located, many others are not. Sometimes one particular practitioner of the occult acquires a great reputation, as a result of which far more people want to consult with him or her than with lesser known practitioners. This can be very frustrating, as the waiting lines are very long at times.

Under the circumstances, people interested in "readings" in rural areas frequently form their own private circle, with one of their number serving as the amateur medium. Frequently, two friends start out working a Ouija board in order to learn things about the future, others stick to the time-honored tea leaves, coffee grounds, or tarot cards.

Undeniably, our educational system does not allow much room for the occult, mysticism, or any form of the irrational. While European education does not necessarily include such subjects or sanction their study, the environment supplies activities in these areas as a matter of course. There is simply less prejudice against the possibility of an occult world among foreign-born or first generation Americans than among the rest of the population, except in the case of American Indians and to some degree Black Americans. There does not seem to be any particular preponderance of national backgrounds among professional psychics one way or another. Nearly all nationalities and religious backgrounds are represented among those I have personally investigated.

As far as private individuals practicing some form of occultism is concerned, there is always a potential conflict with the individual's religious persuasion, if that individual is an orthodox practitioner of it. Many of those who have had psychic experiences, or who seek them, find themselves in a quandary if they are strict Roman Catholics, orthodox Protestants or Jews. In some cases, they will suppress or ignore their psychic interests out of fear that they might endanger their soul! In other cases, they will ask for advice whether or not they were in fact hurting their spiritual development by engaging in psychic work. Naturally, being psychic or following a course of studies in the field in no way endangers a person's spiritual standing; if anything, it contributes to it. If it were not for the facts discovered by modern parapsychology, the religious establishment would not have a single leg to stand upon. Ultimately, the scientific methods of parapsychology and the emotional path of religious faith will merge to provide man with a single image of the deity principle.

If you are living in an area in which you do not have access to professional psychics or other occult practitioners and desire to avail yourself of such services, you may do well in joining up with similarly minded persons and form a *home circle*. Three or more people are sufficient, and it is important that meetings be held on the same day each week to establish a rhythmical continuity. Once the rhythm is broken, whatever psychic powers have been accumulated by the meetings until that point will be lost again, and the work must begin from square one.

The home circle should appoint one of their members as secretary who will take down everything that happens during the sessions. This may include not only the actual communications, if any, or impressions while some member of the circle is in a state of reception, or even trance, as sometimes happens, but also fleeting and minor thoughts that may occur to the members of the group from the moment of their meeting onward. In retrospect, the journals of such meetings contain valuable material, and frequently bits and pieces of information not thought of as significant at the time turn out to be extremely evidential in retrospect. In fact, the proceedings of a home circle should be reviewed by the participants once a month to see how much of the material has already become objective reality. Naturally, home circles do not exist for the purpose of divining the future exclusively. Much time is also spent on communication with the so-called dead, during which relatives, friends, or just strangers let the circle members know of their existence in another dimension, frequently tell them about themselves, and just as frequently turn into advisors for the living, predicting events and warning of impending problems. When this is done in the spirit of exploration, taking the communicators with more than a grain of salt, it is a fine way of delving into the occult world, of deriving benefits from one's activities, and, especially if the communications are genuine and turn out to be evidential, of major benefit to some member of the circle or their friends. But care should be taken that this does not become an addiction; when the advice of discarnates is sought in every detail of daily life, when the dead are asked the most trivial questions by the living, and when the advice from the communicators becomes the norm in the lives of those seeking their help, then the home circle has turned into a crutch. Such a crutch is an unhealthy thing because it deprives the living of their sacred right—and duty—of decision making. Under the karmic law, opportunities and situations are thrust at us so that we may make the right decision. If we follow the counsel of a discarnate advisor blindly, without weighing it, just because it comes to us from that source, we are in fact depriving ourselves of a major part of personality. It should also be recalled that some communicators, though existing in the dimension generally referred to as spiritual, are by no means superior to us in judgment or knowledge.

If there is a home circle with an established communicator or guide, great care should be taken not to expect yes and no answers to leading questions. Whether the means of communication is a Ouija board, of which I have written before, and which I do not particularly like, or the tarot cards, or a crystal ball, or table tipping, or just straight clairvoyance, the bulk of the information must come from the other side of life. Asking questions, in which definite information is given as well, in the expectation of receiving a yes or no reply is simply fooling yourself. Even if the answer turns out to be correct in the long run, the likelihood of its having been given by a discarnate entity is not very great. It should be remembered that our own unconscious can be tapped during home circles in exactly the same way we establish communication with another dimension. But if general questions are put to the discarnate entity communicating, asking simply for information concerning a person or concerning a period in time, the burden of truth lies on the communicator in the next dimension, who then must give details from his or her own knowledge. This becomes especially evidential if the answers contain elements unknown to all those in the circle. If such information subsequently turns out to be correct, the unconscious of the sitters can then be ruled out as a source of that information.

While telepathy may be an astounding process to outsiders, it is nevertheless a common occurrence in the psychic world. Telepathy between living people, whether between amateurs or between amateur and amateur medium, is frequently the source of information in home circles, and while it is desirable and remarkable, in no way does it prove spirit communication in such cases. The only material that truly can be said to emanate from individuals in other dimensions than the physical one must be detailed as to names, places, and circumstances, and must be totally unknown to all those present in the circle at the time the information is received. It is not always easy to establish what is known and what is unknown to the sitters. In order to avoid self-delusion, sitters should examine the material in the light of their earlier experiences through the years, even going back into childhood, to determine whether or not this information could have been known to them, consciously or unconsciously. Only if such possibilities have been rigorously excluded, can a communication obtained in the home circle be labeled as truly derived from spiritual sources.

As a sort of school, there is little difference in value between a home circle and a professional circle sitting for "spiritual development" as it is conducted by many Spiritualist mediums. Naturally, if the professional Spiritualist medium is very strong, that will make the development classes also more effective; but I have found that most home circles eventually develop one stronger member, if indeed they do not start with one, who then becomes the leading individual, the amateur medium of the circle. Whether or not the circle is successful in raising the psychic abilities of the individual members depends upon the period of time during which the same members of the circle meet, the regularity of the meetings, and their congeniality. Unquestionably, the sum total of the psychic powers in each individual is higher when they stay together for a period of time. Why this is so, we do not fully know; some element other than the purely mathematical addition of the psychic potentials of the individuals involved enters the picture, making the overall power that much greater. Some home circles like to keep a religious image by starting with a prayer and ending with one. If the members of the circle are religiously oriented, this will help them relax and perhaps establish a sense of security in that the prayer may keep out undesirable elements from the spiritual world. The prayer itself has no magic powers; it is the belief put into them that creates the thought forms and feelings of impact. Thus, it is entirely conceivable that a Pagan incantation in lieu of a Christian prayer would have exactly the same results for the sitters, if they happen to be Pagans. Popular misconceptions to the contrary, home circles for spiritual development or psychic work do not meet in darkened rooms, with black drapes covering all windows. The need to exclude daylight exists solely in attempts at materializations, when white light could be destructive to any ectoplasmic form produced with the help of the sitters. Other than for materializations, darkness is totally unnecessary. On the other hand, glaring electrical lights do set up disturbing magnetic vibrations that can interfere with the success of the circle. Consequently, it is best to have relaxing, somewhat subdued lighting, or just daylight. In fact, a circle may meet outdoors in the garden, if the climate allows and noise is absent. Any form of loud noise, especially that produced by electromagnetic machinery, can be destructive to the harmony of the circle as well as to the results.

The room in which a home circle meets should be well ventilated, and some air should be allowed to enter at all times. The less noisy it is, the better. Seats should be comfortable, and it may be necessary to have water handy as dehydration accompanies most psychic attempts. There is no need for special clothing when working in a home circle, but the more comfortable and relaxed one is, the better for the results. Smoking and drinking are definitely out during or immediately before a circle meeting. It isn't wise to attempt a circle immediately after a major meal. Needless to say, any form of drug taking is not only destructive to the results of a home circle, but also incompatible with any form of psychic work. This includes LSD and "grass." As I pointed out in *Psycho-Ecstasy*, there are other ways of getting "high" than by artificial stimulation from drugs.

There are people who cannot find like-minded individuals to form even the smallest home circle and yet desire to involve themselves in psychic communication or studies. Reading the literature, watching films dealing with the subject, and other indirect ways of involvement will never take the place of personal development. Practically everybody can develop to the point of being their own medium. The sole exception would be a mentally deficient individual, someone under medical treatment for a major disease, whether organic or nervous, or a person so deeply convinced of a skeptical position that he or she would block any attempt to develop within themselves. The average individual can induce a higher degree of receptiveness through a series of attitudes and some very simple techniques.

The attitude has to be one of receptiveness, that is to say, willingness to accept communications from sources in the spiritual dimension, whether these communications are good or bad, not pressing for them at any given time but accepting them when and if they come. One has to convince oneself that the spiritual communication must originate with those on the other side of life; one cannot search them out deliberately and with some specific purpose in mind. So the first important attitude is one of open-mindedness, of acceptance beforehand of anything that might come "through," and not of insistence on answers to specific questions. It is equally important to have a healthy balance between wishful thinking, suggestion, imagination, and that which really transpires within oneself in the way of psychic phenomena. Always seek rational explanations for information obtained, for phenomena observed, before assuming that they belong in the realm of the so-called "supernatural," a term I do not accept as valid, since all psychic phenomena belong well within the range of natural experiences. This is not to say that one should deliberately try to explain away a genuine phenomenon when it occurs, but to exercise all caution when experiencing it.

Several years ago, I was standing in my kitchen making myself some coffee, when all of a sudden I clearly heard a voice near me calling my name. My first thought was that I had imagined it, but then the voice came again, and I knew that it was something close to me yet from a source I could not see. I decided to check whether someone in the apartment might have called out to me. But on checking, I discovered that the only other person in the apartment was my wife, who was at that moment sitting in a chair at the opposite end of the rather large apartment. Had she called out to me I could not have heard it, especially as the door to the kitchen had been closed. Still, I asked whether she had perhaps thought of me and had intended to call me. I assumed, quite rightly, that a telepathic communication could have been taking place between her and me. My wife had not been thinking of me or of calling me at that time. Just the same, I dismissed the matter as of apparently no great consequence. The following afternoon, roughly at the same time, I was again occupied in the kitchen, and once more the voice called out my name, Hans, no more than perhaps one yard from where I was standing. This time I clearly recognized the personality of the caller. Only one person of my acquaintanceship spoke my name in just that manner. Mr. L. H. had passed away rather suddenly sometime before while riding on a bus. He had left his widow in a state bordering on shock. I was quite sure it was he who was reaching out to me for some reason. Immediately I checked the apartment only to find that my wife was in her own room, and the door was closed. Thereupon I telephoned Mr. H.'s widow and found that she was indeed in a state of deep distress. My call helped settle her nerves, and I realized that the communication came at a time when I could play an important part in establishing a link between the late Mr. H. and his widow, possibly preventing her from doing harm to herself.

Once one has established a balanced attitude toward psychic phenomena, and is willing to accept them as and when they come, it is important to establish a rhythm of exercises and not to interrupt that rhythm in order to build up power. The best way to do this is to set aside fifteen to twenty minutes each day, at a time when one is sure to be alone and undisturbed. During that period, one is to sit alone in a quiet room, in as comfortable a position as possible, with eyes closed, mind made as much a blank as possible, and displaying a hopeful, expectant attitude. At first, this will merely be a rest period. Gradually, however, impressions will rise to the surface from the unconscious part of the mind, and it is wise to keep a diary from that point onward. These impressions may concern themselves with past events, either immediately preceding the period of meditation or further back. Some may contain elements that have escaped solution up to that time, while others may be merely symbolic in character. Eventually, matters pertaining to the so-called future will be projected on the inner screen of the mind, and as one continues with these regular periods of exercise, more and more material will project itself, allowing the sitter to develop his paranormal ability in greater and greater measure. After a while, simple and short questions may be "inserted" into the mental computer. The answer will come up in the same manner, allowing for a certain give and take in the process. However, attempts to reach deceased individuals in this way should not be made; the query should be strictly concerning the person directly, concerning a condition or problem, leaving the manner in which the answer is formulated entirely up to the source supplying it, whether that be the person's own unconscious or a discarnate source.

After several weeks, or perhaps months of this, the individual seeker is ready to test his psychic abilities on others. With most people, psychometry is probably the easiest undertaking, that is to say, touching an object belonging to another person and deriving information about that person from it. Test yourself by requesting objects belonging to strangers, and then verify how "accurate" your reading has been. It is less desirable to "read" friends or relatives, since there is usually conscious knowledge of such persons present that would make a proper evaluation of the results more difficult. Depending upon further development, the seeker might experiment with so-called haunted houses, trying to sense a past tragedy in such places and then checking his feelings or findings afterwards with people who might have knowledge of the location involved. At this stage, dream material should also be carefully watched, since psychic communications come frequently in the dream state when the unconscious is more accessible. Self-development should continue even when a certain level of accomplishment has been attained. The more the psychic powers are used, the more they will grow.

7

Spontaneous Phenomena
How to Be an Amateur Ghost Hunter

Frequently, my readers inquire about certain haunted sites described by me in my books, wondering whether they too might visit them. Others have had experiences of their own, haunted houses I know nothing about, but wonder how to proceed in order to get the maximum knowledge from their adventures. On the whole, I do not encourage amateur ghost hunters uncritically, without regard for possible dangers and inconveniences involved. However, there are a number of places that are accessible to the public, where visits are not only possible but encouraged. In the case of private dwellings, it stands to reason that no one is welcome, not even my most avid fans. Also, it should be remembered that the purpose of my investigations is always to dislodge the ghostly entity, not just to gather information as the majority of my colleagues do. As a result, a large percentage of haunted houses I have visited are no longer haunted. There are, of course, those cases in which the initial effort was not successful, there are those cases in which more than one entity exists, and there are those cases in which the haunting is not a ghost personality as such but merely an imprint from the past. Imprints from the past, the result of emotional events, cannot be wiped out by visitors, no matter how many people might come to experience them. Since nearly ninety percent of all ghostly sightings probably fall into the category of psychic imprints rather than ghost personalities, there are a large number of houses and sites where the amateur ghost hunter might indeed experience something along the lines of my own experience, or that of the medium accompanying me on my original visit.

Here are some useful hints on how to visit a haunted house. To begin with, whether this is a place published by me or a house you have heard about from someone else, be sure that there have been recent manifestations, actual witnesses, not just legendary hearsay. There are a great number of marvelous legends about, some of which have substance, others of which do not. I usually require the existence of one or two living witnesses who have actually experienced something out of the ordinary at the specific sites as the minimum requirement for a visit. If you are sure that there are witnesses to phenomena in the place you have chosen for a visit, it is of course useful to know what earlier visitors have experienced there. But you're not likely to get much cooperation from those witnesses if you contact them simply out of curiosity. It takes an extremely generous and friendly person to answer questions from private parties, which is the main reason I generally protect the exact addresses of my witnesses. When you arrive at the house or site, it is wisest not to ask caretakers or others in charge of the premises whether they have seen a ghost. Go inside or visit the site, as if you were sightseeing, gather your own impressions, because the chance of receiving some sort of imprint yourself is considerable. Only after you have spent some time at the spot and have allowed the atmosphere to get to you, and just before leaving, should you make inquiries of those in charge. This is doubly important as you do not want the stories told by caretakers and others on the spot to influence your own perception, if any. Should you be one of those who are sufficiently gifted psychically to actually see or hear a ghostly manifestation, don't turn on your heels and run. The calmer you are, the stronger the impression will be. If the entity addresses you or in some way takes notice of you, speak to it, gather information, whether telepathically or through speech, and observe very carefully all the details of the apparition. Tape recorders are always good to record immediate impressions on the spot, but they do not necessarily pick up telepathic communications, although there are cases on record of that happening. Some public places, especially historical houses, do not permit cameras, but if you are able to take a camera with you, by all means take as many snapshots of the area as you can, preferably without flashbulbs. By pointing your camera into many different directions, you are likely to cover most areas, without any guarantee, however, that you will hit the two dimensional plane in which a particular haunting exists. In the event that your camera turns up "some extras," as spirit photographs are called, be sure that everyone looking at the photographs can plainly see them. Faces and other images that only you can see are most likely clairvoyantly perceived and are not objective psychic photographs. It is particularly important not to imagine things or to read human faces into pictures when there are clearly none visible to the naked eye. All authentic psychic photographs, such as those I have published several years ago in *Psychic Photography—Thresholds of a New Science*, are discernible to everyone, psychic or not.

A number of people are not merely clairvoyant or clairaudient, but clairsentient, meaning they can smell scents of a psychic nature, odors that are not smelt by others at the same time in the same place. Sometimes this manifests as the strong odor of flowers, of perfumes, or even of cigar smoke. These are side manifestations of a haunting and represent some facet of the entity manifesting. Occasionally, people have told me of an eerie experience at a so-called haunted house, stating that an entity had followed them home and had manifested there. However, ghosts simply do not travel. It is possible to free a classical ghost from its prison through the established method of the rescue circle with the help of a trance medium, and by doing so allow the entity the freedom of moving about. Such entities may then attach themselves to their liberators and in this manner manifest from time to time. This has occurred to me over the years when a ghost previously freed by me might "drop in" to let me know that he or she was now doing well. But the likelihood of "picking up" a disturbed entity called a ghost and taking it home with you, if you are not a trance medium, is remote. If disturbances follow the visit to a haunted house, other causes should be considered, such as hypersensitivity to the atmosphere of the house resulting in personal upsets, or plain imagination.

The following pages are a list of some of the most popular haunted houses and sites that can be freely visited by the public.

California

The Whaley House, San Diego, is one of the most haunted mansions in North America. Built in 1857 by Thomas Whaley, an early California pioneer, it is now kept as a museum under the direction of June Reading. It can be visited during the day. Numerous witnesses, including both visitors to the house and the people of San Diego serving as part-time or voluntary guides, have seen ghosts at Whaley House. In particular, the figure of a woman in what used to be a courtroom, the apparition of Thomas Whaley himself, angry at the city of San Diego for having welshed on a contract to lease his house and all sorts of auditory phenomena have been observed. On several occasions the police were called in when the burglary alarm went off, only to find no one inside the house and the upper story windows opened by unseen hands, something that could not have happened except from the inside! Those wishing to read the transcript of a seance held by me with the assistance of Sybil Leek may it find it in an earlier book of mine entitled *Ghosts of the Golden West*. The ghosts have never been sent away, because my investigation wasn't the kind that would have resulted in full liberation. Thus it is entirely possible that one of several ghosts, either the woman, the builder himself, or a child ghost that has also been observed there, might still be found by casual visitors to the Whaley House.

Visitors to San Francisco's Nob Hill may still encounter the elusive specter of a lovely young girl walking up the street, looking neither left nor right, as if she were in a great hurry to get away, which in fact she was. This is the shade of Flora Somerton, who decided to disappear from her palatial mansion hours before she was to wed a wealthy San Francisco gentleman. It happened in 1876, and for many years thereafter they tried in vain to find her. In the end, the parents accepted the medical view that Flora's mind had snapped due to the excitement of the wedding, while in truth she simply did not like the man her parents had picked out for her to marry. Flora was never heard from again until she died broke and sick in a cheap hotel in Montana in 1926. When her body was found, it was dressed in a white ball gown in the fashion of the 1880s. Several reliable witnesses have actually seen her walk up the hill in that very gown. The place to start is California Street, not far from the Fairmount Hotel, uphill, that is to say, on the left side of the street.

The Stage Coach Inn at Thousand Oaks stands not far from Ventura, a few yards back from the main road. Originally, it stood further back but was moved in order to accommodate the improvements. Currently it is run as a museum. The old inn at one time had the reputation of being the kind of hotel people stayed at only if they had to—some never left it alive. But it was a stopover on the old Butterfield Mail route, so business was brisk. Between 1952 and 1965 a number of people have had psychic experiences in the Stage Coach Inn. Sybil Leek accompanied me to the house and reconstructed a story of murder in one of the upper rooms. The Stage Coach Inn can be reached from Los Angeles on the Ventura Freeway in about an hour and a half.

District of Columbia

Probably the most famous haunted mansion in Washington is the Octagon, standing at a busy crossroads and currently the home of the American Institute of Architects. It has recently been restored as a museum and may be visited freely. The Madisons resided in this magnificent mansion at one time, when they were homeless due to the British having burned down the White House in the War of 1812. The Octagon was built by one Colonel John Tayloe in 1800 and boasts at least two female ghosts. One was a servant girl who jumped from the second floor landing to escape the attentions of a British officer, the other was one of Colonel Tayloe's daughters who had brought home an unacceptable man. Not being able to live with her father's disapproval, she jumped or fell to her death, landing on a spot directly underneath the second floor bannister. To this day, phenomena have taken place in the mansion, ranging all the way from footsteps where no one is walking, chandeliers swinging of their own volition, and a carpet mysteriously folding itself back time and again when no one is about. The Octagon can be visited at reasonable hours, but questions about the ghosts are not necessarily answered in the affirmative.

Maryland

A unique opportunity to visit a haunted ship presents itself in Baltimore harbor, where the famous U.S.F. *Constellation* now lies at berth forever. The ship was built in 1797 as the first man-of-war in the United States fleet and eventually was decommissioned by congressional action. After being almost in ruins for a while in Boston, a private committee rescued the old battleship and brought her to Baltimore in 1953. I published a full account of the many hauntings aboard the U.S.F. *Constellation* in *Window to the Past*. The curator, Donald Stewart, as well as a number of visitors, have encountered the ghost of a sailor named Neil Harvey, a man who was blown to bits in punishment for having fallen asleep on duty. In the cruel custom of his day, he was tied to a cannon and sent to kingdom come. The other ghost aboard the U.S.F. *Constellation* is the first captain, Thomas Truxton. He was the one who had ordered the sailor executed in this fashion. The haunted Frigate *Constellation* is available to visitors, and it is just possible that a psychic individual may recapture some of the ghostly events observed by others aboard.

New Hampshire

A famous historical landmark, the Ocean-Born Mary House at Henniker has attracted visitors from all over the country for many years. Now privately owned by Mr. and Mrs. David Russell, the house represents a perfect example of late eighteenth-century work, and is by itself worth a visit. The story goes that a pirate named Don Pedro captured a ship en route to New England, and when he discovered that a baby had just been born to one of the passengers, he became its godfather, and later helped the mother, Mary Wallace, build this magnificent mansion some fifty miles inland. The only stipulation was that he could retire there once he was done with piracy and thus end his days peacefully. Unfortunately, rumors of a treasure that the pirate was said to have brought with him caused a holdup, and in the ensuing duel, the pirate was killed. Over the years, a number of reliable witnesses, including a state trooper, have seen the figure of a tall woman standing by a window looking out onto the road, although at the time there was no one in the house. Others have gone to visit the house and were let in by a strange looking woman who didn't speak very much. When they turned around, the guide was gone, and it was only then that they discovered that they had been taken around the house by a ghost. After a while, pranksters in the area made the Ocean-Born Mary House a target for Halloween nonsense, damaging the house in the process. As a result, the owners began to discount all accounts of a haunting, to the point of denying they were ever in evidence. However, if you wish to visit the Ocean-Born Mary House at Henniker, be assured it has a ghost no matter what the present owners might tell you.

New York

In New York City, there is an area bounded by Forty-fourth and Forty-fifth Streets on one side and Ninth and Tenth Avenues on the other, which has probably half a dozen ghosts still active. The area once served as the potters' field or cemetery for the poor. Clinton Court at 420 West Forty-sixth Street has been the site of a number of hauntings going back to the early nineteenth century, when the back part of the house was Governor Clinton's carriage house. A child ghost, a sailor hanged for mutiny, and a woman, all have been observed in the immediate vicinity. Today, 420 West Forty-sixth Street is an expensive apartment house, and access is possible only to tenants. However, an ingenious visitor might talk the superintendent into letting them walk around the courtyard for a short time.

Up in Washington Heights, at the corner of Edgecombe Avenue and 160th Street, stands a magnificent colonial mansion called the Morris-Jumel Mansion, which is being maintained by the Daughters of the American Revolution as a museum. It can be visited up to four o'clock in the afternoon. Here George Washington made his headquarters during the battle of Long Island, and much history took place. A number of specters have been observed here by reliable witnesses, including a Hessian soldier on the stairs of the third floor, and the restless spirit of Stephan Jumel himself, complaining that he had been done in by his wife, the notorious Betsy Jumel. I have published extensive accounts of the hauntings at the Morris-Jumel Mansion in several of my books. Among the more astonishing phenomena was the appearance to a group of school children of Betsy Jumel wearing a gown that is preserved in one of the showcases upstairs, but that was, of course, totally unknown to the children at the time, since they had not yet entered the place. For reasons of safety, the current committee does not like to talk about ghosts, but you may be assured that there are a number of them still about the Morris-Jumel Mansion.

If you are looking for a haunted church, perhaps St. Mark's in the Bowery, near Tenth Street, in New York City might be of interest. The church was built in 1799, although there is an earlier chapel on record, where Peter Stuyvesant worshipped. The governor himself is buried in the crypt of the present church. About the middle of the nave, a female parishioner has been observed by a number of witnesses, although the church had been closed at the time of the sightings and no one could have been there. Also, heavy footsteps have been heard coming up to the organ loft, and the ghosts, whoever they are, are certainly still in the church. Visits are possible, but as with so many churches these days, it is frequently closed to the public because of vandalism in the neighborhood.

North Carolina

I know of no single haunting with more witnesses to it than the famous Maco light, near Wilmington, North Carolina. This is an old railroad crossing where a light dancing along the tracks has been observed over many years by hundreds of witnesses from all over the country. Some even reported seeing an old railroad lantern dancing at about the height of a human arm, while there are several who have heard the sound of an approaching train when no train was approaching. Today, only an occasional train is run through on this old track. The haunting has its origin in the unfortunate decapitation of one Joe Baldwin, who was riding the caboose of a train when he observed another train bearing down on him. He jumped to the track, frantically swinging his lantern in order to warn the oncoming train, but was killed in the ensuing crash. Those who are in the Wilmington area should go to the track at night, preferably on a moonless night. The likelihood of seeing the Maco light is then very great indeed.

Pennsylvania

Not far from Pittsburgh, in the little town of Millvale, there is a Croatian Roman Catholic church, famous for its excellent frescoes. It is also known as the site of a bizarre haunting. A number of people have seen a figure pass by the altar, when there was no one else in the church. Drafts of cold air have frequently put out the eternal light, and footsteps have also been heard where no one was seen walking. The ghost seems to be the spirit of a priest who served in a wooden church that stood on the same spot prior to the present building. Apparently, the wooden structure burned down, and for some reason, Father Ranzinger, whose church it was, could not let go of the place where he spent all of his life. He attached himself to the new building that went up on the old spot, and I suspect he is still there, walking by the altar at times, looking over the flock.

Canada

If you are ever in Toronto, be sure to visit a Yorkville nightclub called the Mynah Bird; if you do, you will be killing two birds with one stone. The show itself is quite exciting, if you are not prudish. The girls who pose as models for finger painting or who sing and dance are young and attractive, and there is a ghost upstairs who apparently does take a dim view of the proceedings in what used to be an old town house. Some of the girls in the club have seen him, or have heard his footsteps, or have been touched by him. The orchestra found musical instruments moved by themselves, and chairs at times have been thrown into a heap, when minutes before they were standing in rows. The Mynah Bird is open seven evenings a week and can be visited freely, as any nightclub can.

8

Witches and Other Pagans

There is hardly an activity that generates more misconceptions and heated arguments than the subject of witchcraft and the Pagan religious movement today. To the average person, a witch either doesn't exist at all, or is simply something that refers to the Middle Ages and superstition, and therefore belongs in the realm of fairy tales and children's stories. Or, if a witch exists, she is an evil person, doing all sorts of terrible things to innocent children, riding through the air on a broomstick, or sitting at a fireplace with a wart on her nose and a black cat on her shoulder. The stereotype of the witch, a creation of the Middle Ages, is still very much with us. Many motion picture and television producers seem to think that witches look like the fancy caricature bestowed upon humanity by the political church of the fourteenth century, when the "Old Religion" of the peasantry, Paganism, came in conflict with the emerging political power of the Roman Catholic church. I have written extensively on the subject of witchcraft and other Pagan persuasions in three books, the latest of which is called *The Witchcraft Report,* wherein I give details of a number of active groups and individuals in the United

States. Since writing that work, additional studies have been undertaken and new groups have come into being, and material changes have taken place in the groups I knew at the time I researched my earlier book. As a result of this up-to-date information, some appraisals of groups and individuals will have to be altered in the light of current activities, while additional listings are in order and some former listings will have to be omitted.

To sum up the situation, witchcraft in 1974 is not the figment of anyone's imagination. Witchcraft as a term is derived from the Anglo-Saxon word *Wiccacraft,* meaning craft of the wise. It referred to the superior knowledge possessed by certain individuals in a community, knowledge of nature, of herbology, of the natural forces around us, of certain aspects of healing and medicine, and of the ability to contact the deity. Thus, the Wicca was not an evil force at all, but a wise person who was the one individual in the community to whom one could have recourse when religious, medical, or other nonmaterial problems arose. From the beginning of time, the shaman or priest was the wise one, and though the job at first went to a physically handicapped person who could not hunt or fight, eventually it went to the elite of the community and has pretty much remained with the intellectual upper strata. Western witchcraft, a tradition based primarily upon the beliefs of Anglo-Saxon and Scandinavian communities and going back to the Stone Age, is built upon three basic concepts: (1) worship of a female mother goddess principle in lieu of the male god of Christianity; (2) belief in reincarnation and the desire to be born again at the same time and place as the loved ones; and (3) knowledge and working of magic, the term meaning not stage magic but the manipulation of natural law in such a way as to benefit man, to better utilize natural resources, to explore the secrets of the universe, and to discover shortcuts and remedies to improve life. Those are the three cardinal aspects of Wicca. Witches do not believe in the devil,

because the devil came later, being the invention of the
political church of the fourteenth century that needed a tangible adversary to fight in the wake of continuing belief in
Paganism by large sections of the peasantry. The word *devil*
means "stranger" in the Gypsy tongue, but in order to make
this adversary into an Antichrist, the horns of the Greek god
Pan, the goatlike face, plus the fiery aspects of the Phoenician
Beelzebub went into the making of an artificial evil force
called *devil*. That this nonsensical concoction survived seven
hundred years of enlightenment is amazing, but it did. On a
recent television show, a priest who was a fellow guest, and who
had been invited to discuss exorcism with me, insisted in all
seriousness that the devil was a real person, just as described by
holy writ.

Witches do not have familiars, that is to say animals that
they send on errands to do their bidding for them. They may
have domestic animals, because sanctity of all life is part of
the witchcraft belief. Witches do not cast evil spells on unsus-
pecting villagers or townsfolk, but they do heal the sick when
requested to do so. From olden days, witchcraft communities
were essentially agricultural communities, consequently their
rites related to produce and animals. Their fertility rite in
which the female members of the community or coven would
dance around the sacred circle astride broomsticks (symbol of
domesticity), in order to show the grain how high it should
grow, became the fantasy of the broomstick ride through the
sky. The symbolic companion of the mother goddess, called
the horned god, became the devil of the hostile church, just
because the high priest wears a horned helmet during the
ceremonies.

Witchcraft has nothing to do with the Black Mass. The
latter is the invention of sixteenth-century thrill-seekers,
becoming particularly popular in eighteenth-century England.
It is simply a mock-religious service, defiling the Roman
Catholic religion by reversing everything from the crucifix to

the prayers. Since witches do not even acknowledge the existence of Christianity, they would much less want to mock it. Satanism or devil worship has nothing to do with witchcraft either, except that it has borrowed some outer trappings from the witches, perverting the meaning in the process. Where witches worship life and the sanctity of all living creatures, and forbid any form of human or animal sacrifice, where witches believe in doing that which harms no one else, Satanists follow a contrary line of reasoning. Selfishness, greed, lust, and the full satisfaction of sensual desires are not only permitted but also encouraged, destruction of weaker creatures is sanctified, and the principle of egotism praised as a healthy, constructive way of life. It should be stated that *real* satanic groups can no more be covered in a work of this kind than a psychological compendium could deal with mass murderers at large. What passes as satanic worship in the United States is a pale form of self-centered worship, lacking in criminality, and in some instances quite benign. True satanic groups exist all over the world; they are emotionally sick people to whom murder is excitement, who are no more part of the occult scene than the mass murderer is worthy of the tolerance of the community.

In addition to witchcraft covens and individual practitioners, and satanic groups and individuals, there are many forms of Paganism, ranging from revivals of the ancient Egyptian religion to neo-Greek and neo-Celtic forms of worship. What these various groups of different ethnic backgrounds have in common is their Pagan attitude; some are polytheistic and worship a multitude of deities, others are seemingly monotheistic although oriented toward a female supreme being. Some worship in street clothes, and some in black or white robes, some in the nude, and all of them have a deep and growing concern for the sanctity of the environment.

Judging from the amount of mail and inquiries I get every week, there is a rising interest in becoming a Pagan; young people especially seem to be disillusioned with their establishment churches, seeking new religious orientation not out of a desire for a thrilling experience so much as from genuine disillusionment with the religion they were brought up in. Very few seekers ask to be put in touch with the nearest coven of witches to get even with someone, on the assumption that they will learn how to cast an evil spell, practically overnight. Once in a while, someone complains that a neighbor has bewitched them, and they wonder whether they in turn might learn how to bewitch the neighbor. With the rising interest in various forms of Pagan worship, the fanatical wings of the fundamentalist movement have also increased their "vigilance," pouring out tracts and pamphlets against the spreading of what they consider diabolical movements, quoting profusely from the Bible, as if the Bible were indeed directly written by the deity, and in some instances even going so far as to organize "witchmobiles" to propagandize against Satanism throughout the country. The latter development smacks of religious persecution, and in some cases brawls have resulted from provocative behavior on the part of the young fundamentalist fanatics challenging dedicated Pagans not just to debate but to physical fights as well. Since Pagans are not the least bit interested in proselytizing or converting Christians or other religions to their way of life, and are in fact opposed to converts if they do not come from deep and long-lasting conviction, the need for such violent reaction on the part of extremists among fundamentalists hardly seems justified. It is perhaps out of a motive similar to the one that prompted the medieval crusaders to try to wrest the Holy Land from the "infidels" in the misguided notion that Palestine was suffering under the heel of Islam, when in fact Christians, Jews, and Muhammadans lived together quite peacefully.

Today, the Pagan movement is at a crossroads; no longer secret, no longer underground, and fully protected by both federal and state law as an expression of religious convictions, the various Pagan groups, churches, covens, and individuals are free to practice their particular brand of religion as they wish. They are even free to proselytize, if they want to, which they do not. They are not entirely free from social prejudice, and in some outlying communities, ancient superstitions concerning witches and Pagans in general still persist. But by and large very few people are hurt by being Pagans, and in the few cases in which someone has lost a position due to his religious convictions, the courts have been quick in restoring them to their rightful jobs. If anything, the establishment is more than fair to those of unusual religious convictions. The mundane press, on the other hand, always in love with hackneyed clichés, has not changed much in its image of the fantasy witch. Whenever interviews with witches are run, usually on Halloween, they reek of condescension and ridicule, sometimes even to the point of slander. Small wonder then that dedicated practitioners of witchcraft or other Pagan faiths will not permit themselves to be interviewed in the press or on television and radio, preferring to worship quietly or to meet with people of their own convictions. What remains for the public media is a small but vociferous array of would-be witches and warlocks, or whatever fanciful designations they may choose, who no more represent the true Pagan element than the fanatical fundamentalist represents religion. In a recent "survey" in *Esquire* magazine, perhaps a dozen alleged witches and other odd cultists were quoted and shown in their proper habitats. Not one of them had any standing in the Pagan community.

Although the need to secrecy is no longer pressing, another danger already looms large on the horizon of the emerging neo-Pagan movement. As Pagan groups and individuals become free from persecution, they are quick to adapt the methods of conventional religion to their own needs. Splinter groups accuse each other of this and that transgression of the "law," as if there were indeed a written law in Paganism.

Bickering among witches as to who has the proper attitude, accusations answered by other accusations, and intense occupation with words and arguments have become the earmark of many Pagans today. They do no better nor worse than the Christians in this respect, but somehow one would have expected them to do better, because of their proclaimed adherence to the true laws of nature, their love of the environment, and their directness in approaching the supreme power, without the intermediary of a hierarchy or establishment church. To be sure, Paganism is a marvelously positive assertion of man's religious unity with the Creator, but the Pagan establishment is frequently all too human, frequently resembling the Christian establishment in its partisan activities and doctrinal disputes. While this may not be Paganism's downfall, it has certainly retarded its universal acceptance.

In the following pages, I will list those Pagan groups and individuals who are accessible to seekers, both for information and possible initiation. It should be kept in mind that subscription to a Pagan journal may be an easy thing, but acceptance into an active group is not. In some strict groups, a year and a day of apprenticeship is needed before even a rudimentary initiation is proffered. In others, acceptance depends upon individual merit and characteristics. There is no way in which one can force oneself into the group; there is no way to buy oneself in. Membership in a witchcraft coven or other Pagan community does not confer magical powers upon the new member, but in time leads to the most important accomplishment of witchcraft—as Dr. Leo Martello, the New York witch, has so aptly put it, mastery over self. Anyone who expects a witch to turn an enemy into a toad is an idiot. Involvement with a Pagan religion is primarily for the purpose of personal unfoldment, not for the purpose of influencing others.

In many Pagan groups, initiates take secret names by which

they are known to each other. This is based upon an old belief that there is power not only in individual letters but also in names and entire sentences. Consequently, changing from the mundane name to the Pagan name separates the world of the material from the world of the spiritual. It is expected that the secret name not be used with outsiders, but lately a number of coven leaders have freely used it while trying to cover up their real names. This seems deplorable, if, as these leaders state, they wish to acquaint the broad public with their Pagan culture and beliefs. The time for secrecy is long past, and if the Pagan movement has nothing to hide, then it should include the mundane names and occupations of those who practice the various ancient faiths. I do not believe that anyone can be fired from his job because he follows a Pagan religion. If such action were taken, and occasionally it happens, reinstatement is swift. There is nothing in any of the Pagan faiths, including even the Satanism practiced in the United States, that is in any way dangerous to the community or an overt invitation to political rebellion.

The following Pagan groups are by no means all of those practicing their particular religion at this time, but they do represent the majority, and all of those I have personally come in contact with. It is in the nature of Pagan groups in general that they come together and dissolve rather frequently, being far more ephemeral than Christian or other religious communities are. People get together for a reason, group themselves around a particular leader or ideal, and when they are tired of it, or find their leader to have feet of clay, they drift away and find new outlets for their religous expression.

Why do people want to be witches? Why do people want to be known as Pagan in a world in which Christianity, Islam, Judaism, Buddhism, and half a dozen other major religions hold nearly all the trump cards? Some do it out of sincere conviction, truly motivated by emotional needs or expressing their religiosity in such a manner. For them none of the other religions will do, simply because they do not suit their individual needs. While the number of such truly sincere Pagans is not more than a few thousand in this country, they are the ones who will ultimately carry the Pagan movement forward into full respectability and acceptance by the world community. There are far larger numbers of disgruntled Christians, Jews, Muhammadans, etc., who are simply discontented with their own religion or upbringing and seek a new way toward God. From their negative feelings can come some very positive things, if they realize that a Pagan religion is by no means a free-for-all, or a field to express license and abandonment. Religion is religion, whether Christian or Pagan. There are some people who turn to Paganism because they expect from it erotic or unconventional excitement, because of thrills of doing something forbidden, at least forbidden by their own church, and out of a desire to involve themselves in what they consider secret and mysterious. But there are a very large number of people who turn toward some form of Pagan religion because of boredom with themselves, with the lives they are forced to lead by the social system we have in this country, or for that matter in this world, who seek out witchcraft and other Pagan cults as the only means of escaping anonymity and an existence that has neither challenge nor thrill for them. These people love the secrecy of their newly found faiths, making a great deal of it, and sometimes going to great extremes to stress the superiority of their newly found religious convictions. Not infrequently, they turn into fanatics for what they consider a good cause. When such people infiltrate bona fide Pagan communities and become powerful in them, the quality of Pagan worship suffers as a result, partly because the *genuine* Pagan is a peaceful and retiring individual, and partly because of the infiltrator's constant need for self-reassurance through strident extroverted display of custom, dress, and ritual.

The following pages are a listing of covens and other Pagan communities, arranged alphabetically by state.

Alaska

Anchorage, Alaska is the site of a useful and active coven with special emphasis on healing services. "Do you realize that your book, *The Witchcraft Report*, is the most informative on the market concerning the Craft?" the high priestess, Mrs. Mia LaMoureaux, wrote to me recently. "Our work is to educate the youth in the Old Ways. At present, we have an Outer Circle coven of young people who meet once a week at our home for classes and also on the full moon for esbats. They are being taught to be tomorrow's teachers, and I will never cease to be amazed at the openness and understanding displayed by these young people. Wicca has opened a whole new area of interest, and the enthusiasm it has caused in their lives is something akin to a whole group of 'John the Baptists' of the Old Religion." Mrs. LaMoureaux has lectured and appeared on television, and has opened her home to those in trouble in any way. Those interested in Wicca, the Anglo-Saxon form of witchcraft, may contact Mrs. Mia LaMoureaux at: Post Office Box 8151, Anchorage, Alaska 99508. **Recommended.**

Arizona

Ernest Bidwell is the head of a small traditionalist coven, and editor of a newsletter called *The Silver Ankh*, which appears quarterly. By profession a writer, he has recently moved to Arizona from Redlands, California, where he headed a small Outer Circle Court coven as priest. "I am a traditionalist witch," Mr. Bidwell stated to me. "Though not a Gardnerian, I am a great admirer of the late Gerald B. Gardner and the work he did for the Craft. I believe the United States will be 'the future renaissance for the Craft and Paganism in general.' " Mr. Bidwell permits me to publish a sample of his witchcraft poetry.

"Oh goddess of magic end of the moon, of Eve's twilight evening and shining star, of the darkened night in mystery enchanted realms, of beyond, and restful sleep, and misty dreams. That silvery maid of woodland glade, oh sacred is her name, by stone altar, her image, or candle flame."

Ernie Bidwell may be reached at 565 Howard Drive, N.E., Sierra Vista, Arizona 85635. **Recommended.**

California

The greatest Pagan leader and intellectual pioneer today is Fred Adams, artist, cinematographer, social scientist, and archaeologist. Those of my readers who recall an earlier book, *The New Pagans,* will also recall my chapter dealing with Feraferia, the organization created and headed by Fred Adams, and they may recall the marvelously colorful jacket of that book, also the work of Fred Adams. The Paganism of Feraferia is a blend of ancient Cretan wisdom, Greek traditions, Celtic ritual, and the Fairy Faith, all of it seen through the eyes of the truly idealistic seeker. Some of the ritual and literature of Feraferia is highly involved and sophisticated; those looking for quick initiation and easily assimilated magic will not find it here, but those looking for the deeper mysteries —emotional, physical, and environmental involvement of self in the very forces of nature—will find the path of Feraferia not only stimulating but also unequaled in the world of religious experiences.

Feraferia accepts individuals for membership when they come recommended by other members or their demonstrated works in the world. The organization publishes a small magazine called *Korythalia,* written to a large extent by Frederic MacLaurin Adams himself, and illustrated by his hand.

Together with his lady, Svetlana, Fred Adams lives a quiet life, dispensing ancient wisdom and rediscovering long forgotten truths. To Fred Adams, everything rests upon the position of the calendar, thus astrology and a deep knowledge of natural law are essentials in understanding the Pagan way of life. The magazine *Korythalia* can be subscribed to, and inquiries concerning membership in Feraferia received at: Post Office Box 691, Altadena, California 91001. **Recommended.**

Sara Cunningham is an enormously gifted teacher of Wicca, a witchcraft high priestess with a New England background, specializing in herbs, aromatics, oils, and teachings of the Craft. Until recently, she held classes in witchcraft at her rambling old house in Pasadena, but she has now removed to Oregon, where she has built for herself and her followers a rural covenstead. However, she and her associates still run an occult supply shop called Stonehenge, where occult tools, oils, perfumes, publications, and information is being dispensed. Those wishing to contact Sara Cunningham can do so at: Post Office Box 204, Wolf Creek, Oregon 97497. **Recommended.**

Fred and Martha Adler, originally from the Midwest, have a small coven of traditional witches in the Hawthorne area of greater Los Angeles. Martha Adler specializes in teaching. She may be contacted at: 4501 West 141st Street, Hawthorne, California 90250. **Recommended.**

Cassandra Salem is a teacher of witchcraft in the Huntington Beach area who heads a coven numbering several dozen people from all walks of life. The wife of a prominent professional man, Cassandra, whose civilian name is Mrs. Judy Malis, is not ashamed to discuss her Pagan philosophy, and has appeared in the public press and on television to express her views. **No comment.**

The Church of The Eternal Source is a place where you can

practice the ancient Egyptian religion the way it was practiced several thousand years ago, if that is your bent. It is presently presided over by a civil engineer, Harold Moss, a man with a full beard and long brown hair who walks about in a colorful striped caftan. He is described as "nervous, fidgety," and in a statement especially prepared for this publication, explains that "his job is to be visible, but he is definitely not the spiritual *leader* of the Egyptian church." Nevertheless, he is powerful in this particular movement, although there are several others with him, and there is even a subdivision of this particular Pagan church in New England. The church provides information and instruction about the goddess and gods in general, Egyptian things, and various occult techniques. "We support and teach the unity and harmony of existence, the basic ideal that all beings, all things, are to be approached in joy and reverence in order to gain understanding and wisdom. We are ecology oriented because of the Egyptian teaching that all beings are interrelated and balanced, that each being and thing must be treated with respect to its individuality, and terms of its relationship to other things. We teach that it is each person's responsibility to work out his or her own karma and that the goddesses and gods do not remove any of one's; he has responsibilities to correct errors and to do better next time, both in this life and in others. The goddesses and gods aid one in becoming more human, in discovering more, in experiencing more, they do not do it for one." To this beautiful ideal, Harold Moss adds a voice of warning. "It is true that right now the law in the United States is religious toleration, but we must never take that for granted. Many mystics see a time of persecution beginning in 1980 or shortly thereafter. Books will be burned, and many will die."

Mr. Moss then states the Egyptian credo as follows: "Thou Art God. So long as you harm no one, do as you will. Know yourself as above, so below."

Mr. Moss warns against the use of drugs saying: "Those

who think they have to take drugs to reach a religious experience are mistaken. Religion is the most natural, most healthy, most ordained condition of the human mind."

As the result of a long and bitter infight between various factions of an organization called the Council of Themis, the Pagan camp has been split in two lately. The Council of Themis, named after an Aegean goddess of very ancient lineage, was a roof organization of various Pagan groups, primarily the brainchild of Fred Adams and a few likeminded individuals. Two groups, one in England and one in San Francisco, who used drugs and blatant sex in their rituals, were finally expelled from the council, as a result of which there ensued what I called, "the war of the witches" in my book *The Witchcraft Report*. After protracted arguments back and forth, some of the members of the council walked out and formed their own organization called the Council of Earth Religions, with Harold Moss and Stephen Bell as chief administrators. In essence, there is little difference between the two organizations except personalities. Unfortunately, the Reverend Harold Moss and his group felt that they were being slighted by the account I gave of the infighting in the Pagan camp, and so they issued a "corrective" memorandum, setting down their side of the dispute. Anyone reading this memorandum will wonder whether the Pagan movement has really come of age, or whether perhaps most of its time is spent in doctrinal bickering on minor points precisely the way the emerging Christian church did in the fourth century A.D. Since the memorandum circulated by the Council of Earth Religions repudiated some statements made to me by the Reverend Carroll Runyon, Grand Master of the O.T.A. and a leading Council of Themis member at the time, I took up the matter again with Mr. Runyon. But Mr. Runyon stuck to his guns—he had told me the truth, as he saw it, and as it appeared, and had no corrections to make.

"It is not I who am admirable, but my faith," Mr. Moss

states. "Actually all this publicity is damaging my personal growth, and I look forward to the day when someone else can do this job, and I can concentrate on more personal goals." Those interested in the Church of the Eternal Souce, which practices the ancient Egyptian religion, may inquire at: Post Office Box 7091, Burbank, California 91510. The church welcomes new members and offers interesting teachings, colorful rituals, and an unusual slant on religious expression. **Recommended.**

The aforementioned O.T.A. is a Hermetic-Rosicrucian lodge in the Western occult tradition, the letters standing for Ordo Templi Ashtart. "Our theurgy derives from the clavicles of Solomon and the Kabbalistic system of the Order of the Golden Dawn. Without embracing the 'law of Thelema,' we adhere to the Gnostic tradition of the Ordo Templi Orientis through the dispensation of the late senior advisor, the venerable Louis T. Culling. Our order is sponsored by the Church of Hermetic Science, a California religious corporation chartered on October 23, 1970. The church is non-denominational, does not proselytize a dogma or revelation. The O.T.A. is secret and initiatory but not clandestine."

The order maintains a main lodge in Pasadena and a lodge in Pittsburgh, Pennsylvania. At the heart of this group lies the practice and study of "Ceremonial Magick," which is described as an art, rather than a science, involving, as it does, man's creative imagination. The O.T.A. also publishes a magazine called *The Seventh Ray,* which contains both practical and highly involved articles on the subject of Magick, the Order, and technical material. It is written, to a large extent, and superbly illustrated by the very talented Grand Master Frater Aleyin, in private life Carroll Runyon, writer, illustrator, and scientist. Those wishing to study Magick, medieval demonology, and the mastering of the inner planes of man may find O.T.A. to their liking. Information may be obtained by contacting O.T.A. at: Post Office Box 3341, Pasadena, California 91103. **Recommended.**

The Light of Truth Church, headed by Nelson H. White, and connected with "The Magick Circle" shop, is an "unstructured Order, offering classes in magick." Post Office Box 3125, Pasadena, California 91103. **No comment.**

The Ordo of Thelema is the name of a small group centering around one Stephen Bell, member of the Council of Earth Religions. Address: 4445 Thirty-sixth Street, San Diego, California 92116. **No comment.**

The Church of Wicca at Bakersfield is the result of much hard work on the part of George Patterson, who came here from Maryland where he was originally initiated into witchcraft. Describing themselves as a Celtic group, the Church of Wicca is a traditional coven, consisting of George Patterson and a number of young people in the area. Mr. Patterson is also an ordained minister of the Universal Life Church and holds the degree of doctor of divinity. At the beginning, he referred to his group as Georgians and stated his aims to include: "the worship of the Old Religion, to aid members to progress and improve themselves mentally, physically, and spiritually, and to work Magick for the benefit of its members and for any others who may seek it out for aid, for right purposes." Those living in the area may wish to contact George Patterson at: Church of Wicca, 1908 Verde Street, Bakersfield, California 93304. **Recommended.**

When I researched *The Witchcraft Report,* I referred to a group of comparatively recent origin called Nemeton. I quoted the official statement by its leaders to the effect that they were "Pagans who had joined together, believed in many gods, many ways." *Nemeton* is an ancient Celtic word meaning "grove" or "sanctuary of Pagans." The founders of Nemeton have obtained a secluded 220-acre site, *Coeden Brith,* which is

Welsh for "Speckled Forest," with hills, fields, groves, streams, and wild grapes and mistletoe among the oaks. Since that time I have gotten to know the organization and some of its members a lot better and am forced to reevaluate my original enthusiastic opinion. The piece of land referred to in the original statement does indeed exist, provided for the organization by a certain Lady Cynthia a few years ago. After a disagreement with the cofounder of the group, Tom DeLong, Cynthia, a lovely, tall woman of gentle persuasion, left Oakland, California, and Nemeton for Florida, where she has been ever since, no longer connected with the group. Leadership then fell upon the aforementioned Mr. DeLong, and the pudgy, hard-working individual using the name of Alison Harlow. Together, with the help of some like-minded individuals, they managed to publish a beautiful magazine called *Nemeton*, also containing articles, poems, and even Pagan songs written by Mr. DeLong, poet Poul Anderson, Victor H. Anderson, and others. The magazine was so well produced physically that it was no great surprise when it ran into financial difficulties before long, lacking general public acceptance.

In addition to the overall organization called Nemeton, the group worked in a private coven of Welsh tradition called Cenedl, membership to which was and is restricted to those the two coleaders accept. The rituals contain some very picturesque and ancient traditions. "We believe that the Lady is regent of the year, all the seasons, while the consorts are twofold, a bull god and a stag god, whose attributes are the waning and waxing year," Mr. DeLong, who uses the Welsh name of Gwydion Pendderwen, explained.

As so often happens with successful groups, whether Pagan or Christian, there came a time when Nemeton was no longer satisfied to offer a forum for divergent Pagan groups in the San Francisco area but felt more and more that it should be the arbiter and defender of all Pagan causes in California, whether called upon to do so or not. As a result, the group entered the bickering foray in the various Pagan newsletters in full force, thereby degrading their original high purpose as envisioned by Lady Cynthia. At a recent meeting with this group, half a dozen individuals showed up including the two leaders, Tom DeLong, Alison Harlow, Joseph Wilson of St. Louis, Aidan Kelly, and Isaac Bonevits.

And who are these people? Mr. Thomas DeLong, alias Gwydion Pendderwen, is a former Internal Revenue Service agent, currently said to be working for the Department of Health, Education and Welfare in the San Francisco area.

Alison Harlow, coleader, according to a Californian active in the Pagan movement who knows her, "is more interested in politics, especially the women's liberation movement, and is like a little ball of fire which goes in all directions."

Aidan Kelly is a retiring, slight young man, self-described as a "black priest" of a coven in the San Francisco area. "This is based on the old perverted idea that Satan appeared to the medieval witches as a black man," my California informant explained. Mr. Kelly has a small organization called the New Reformed Orthodox Order of the Golden Dawn. However, the real Order of the Golden Dawn, based upon the great traditions of the 1890s, has nothing to do with Mr. Kelly or his organization.

Isaac Bonevits is a young writer from Berkeley whose main claim to fame has been a book entitled *Real Magic*, as well as a widely circulated statement that he is the first and only person who ever received a bachelor's degree in magic. However, according to the registrar of the University of California, Berkeley, Mr. Bonevits received a B.A. degree as a student in the College of Letters and Science, where his major was magic. The degree, however, is not "in magic."

Apparently, Mr. Bonevits's interests extended to the infamous Psychedelic Venus Church of San Francisco, the very same that had been read out of the Council of Themis and had started all the ruckus because of their insistence on the use of drugs and blatant sex in the service.

When I attempted to interview the head of that organization, he referred me to the "Reverend" Isaac Bonevits as the man in charge who could satisfy my curiosity. It turned out that Mr. Bonevits could not help; instead, he gave me the telephone number of a woman who in turn might know where the former head of the Psychedelic Venus Church might be at that time. In a recent edition of the Pagan newspaper *Earth Religion News*, published in Brooklyn, New York, there is an article entitled "Will the Real Isaac Bonevits Please Sit Down."

Apparently, the precocious youngster has dabbled in a number of occult practices, having sought entry into Satanism, only to be personally removed in the end by the head of that Church, Anton LaVey, despite the plea to be permitted to stay in the organization. In recent months, Mr. Bonevits has turned into a Druid, but, according to expert Dr. Leo Martello, he is definitely not a witch.

As for Mr. Joseph Wilson of St. Louis, he is the same gentleman who went quietly to England some time back when a furor arose over his disclosed identity as an informer for the United States Army, having put the finger on alleged antiwar demonstrators among the military in Vietnam. Mr. Wilson has since returned to the United States. At one time, he published a newsletter called *The Waxing Moon*.

Those still wishing to investigate Nemeton for themselves, may do so by contacting the organization at: Post Office Box 13037, Station E, Oakland, California 94661. Telephone: 415-339-8362. **Not recommended.**

Nelly Heathen is the title of a periodical dedicated to living Paganism, as seen through the eyes of the Psychedelic Venus Church of Berkeley, California. The newspaper in front of me shows a couple copulating atop an altar between two lighted candlesticks. Sex, nudity, the use of marijuana, although not of stronger drugs, and great personal freedom are stock and trade of this organization, which may be classed as politically radical. It is not, however, lacking in sincerity in its own beliefs and convictions, and the newspaper contains a number of interesting articles on the worship of the Goddess Kali, and other forms of Paganism that the Psychedelic Venus Church equates with its own way of life. This is certainly not for the average seeker, and there are those who will say that it is tending to be pornographic at times. But like it or not, it is the genuine expression of a group of people, living their own way of life, not seeking converts or otherwise making a public nuisance of themselves. Their manifesto says in part: "We work as part of the spiritual and cultural revolution sweeping the universe, the free and humanistic affirmation of people instead of systems, governments, and machines, of pleasure instead of aggression. We choose the Mediterranean sex goddess Venus Aphrodite as our symbol of hedonic pleasure. We will do what we can to prevent warfare, racism, sexism, and ecological disaster." In a statement to me, Jefferson Clitlick also complained of writer Susan Roberts' implication of a link between the Psychedelic Venus Church and any form of Satanism. "That is plain libel," Mr. Clitlick explained. Those wishing to learn more about this unusual group may write to: Psychedelic Venus Church, Post Office Box 4163, Sather Gate Station, Berkeley, California 94704. **Not recommended.**

Anton LaVey has become the best-known Satanic priest in the United States, if not the world, because of his shrewd sense of public relations and a great flair for showmanship, which is evident to anyone visiting his headquarters in San Francisco. Mr. LaVey has had several careers, as a police photographer, as a lion tamer in a circus, and now as the high priest of the First Satanic Church of California, wearing the collar of the clergyman for interviews and the devil's costume for rituals. Mr. LaVey is also a superb organist and a better than average painter, and all in all, a pleasant, somewhat soft-spoken fellow. His philosophy is another matter. The way he sees it, there is no actual devil, but the devil within all of us should be encouraged, meaning lust, selfishness, and greed. Some have compared his point of view to neo-fascism, while others find it an outlet for suppressed hostilities in those unable to cope with their own problems. Rituals at Mr. LaVey's headquarters are colorful and exciting, although it should be borne in mind that modern Satanism is a heresy of witchcraft, borrowing some of the outer trappings of the "Old Religion," but perverting all of its meanings. Due to the success of his original venture in San Francisco, Mr. LaVey's Satanic Church has spread out and established "grottoes" in various parts of the United States. The success of these subdivisions inevitably led to strife within the organization, resulting again in some groups splitting off and going their own way, after denouncing Mr. LaVey as a dictator. Mr. LaVey has written a number of books, and has appeared on the cover of national magazines. He is by no means the devil incarnate, nor is he a dangerous man. His philosophy corresponds to much of the evil within us in this destructive age, and it is for that reason that it may find a number of adherents. Those wishing to acquaint themselves with Satanism as practiced by Anton LaVey will find his headquarters on California Street, San Francisco, California. **Not recommended.**

Delaware

One of many groups loosely tied together under the name the Pagan Way, headquarters at Wilmington, Delaware, but the group concentrates most of its activities in the Philadelphia area. The Pagan Way is a fellowship of Pagans, worshiping the forces of nature, and not necessarily calling themselves witches. But the difference is one of degree, not kind. Many members of Wicca are also members of one of the subdivisions of the Pagan Way. Those wishing to know more about the activities and publications of this group, may contact: John Wootten, the Pagan Way, Post Office Box 2015, Wilmington, Delaware 19899. **Recommended.**

Florida

The Black Light is the name of a poorly written newsletter filled with diatribes of a partisan nature, occasionally carrying pieces on the Celtic aspects of the Craft. It is published by one Kitty Lessing, who calls herself the Hollywood Coven and who may be reached by those in the area at: Post Office Box 1179, Hollywood, Florida 33022. **Not recommended.**

Those whose interest lies in pursuing the studies of Satanism will find a "grotto" of the Satanic Brotherhood, which is the split-off part of Anton LaVey's organization, at St. Petersburg, Florida. The priest in charge is Harry L. Booth: Post Office Box 10373, St. Petersburg, Florida 33714. **No comment.**

Illinois

The Sabaean Temple in Chicago, headed by Frederico de Arechaga, Rex Sacrorum, is an elaborate Pagan establishment, following in the main along the lines of the ancient Babylonian traditions of witchcraft. Mr. de Arechaga also runs a selective occult shop called El Sabarum, where inquiries about the Sabaeans may be made. Rituals vary widely from highly secret to open, just as the worshipers include the very young, even family groups, all the way up to people in their sunset years. During most rituals, the worshipers wear street clothes while the temple staff is dressed in long robes. The erotic element is not particularly stressed in those rituals open to the public but can be quite exciting in the closed rituals open only to higher initiates. There are temple dancers and musicians, superbly trained by the high priest, who also furnishes the original music and who has been responsible for most of the decorations. If and when Mr. Arechaga ever passes into the next state of existence, he will undoubtedly be elevated to a Pagan deity, having already earned so many credits while here on earth. Address: El Sabarum, 2553 North Halsted, Chicago, Illinois 60614. **Recommended.**

Maryland

Morgana is a lady with a small coven in Baltimore, worshiping in the traditional Wicca way, which is to say "skyclad," nude, following pretty much along the lines of Alexander Sanders of England. This is a small coven of quiet, unassuming people. Those in the area interested may contact: Mary Davis, Post Office Box 4818, Baltimore, Maryland 21211. **Recommended.**

Massachusetts

Witch Tarun is the attractive lady who runs a coven at South Lancaster, Massachusetts, and also publishes a mimeographed newsletter called *Word to the Wise.* She is a hereditary witch and her coven worships in the Anglo-Saxon persuasion. The coven may be contacted at: Box 139, South Lancaster, Massachusetts 01561. **Recommended.**

In the Boston area there is the "Du Bandia Grasail" Coven, following along the lines of Alexander Sanders of England. These worshipers of the Wicca number about a dozen at present, meet once a week in Boston, and occasionally hold seasonal ceremonies outside the city. They work in the nude. The group also studies the works of many philosophers, the kabbalah, and is liberal in its views. Those interested may contact the coven at: Box 43, Allston, Massachusetts 02134. **Recommended.**

Minnesota

Around the personality of Carl Weschke and Lady Sheba, there exists an entire establishment of witchcraft publications, activities, lectures, and teaching seminars. Most of the writing appears in *Gnostica News*, and Llewellyn Publications publishes a large number of books and pamphlets dealing with various aspects of the occult. While this house is not quite on a par with commercial trade publishers, they make up in enthusiasm what they lack in professionalism. Witchcraft is alive and well in Minneapolis. Anyone interested in witchcraft activities in the area should contact: Llewellyn Publications, Box 3383-GN, St. Paul, Minnesota 55165. **No comment.**

Missouri

The Church of All Worlds is a neo-Pagan organization with "nests" or subdivisions in various other places in the United States. Its philosophy is based primarily upon the science fiction work of Robert Heinlein, *Stranger in a Strange Land*. Since its inception, the organization has come a long way toward balancing its views toward a more mature point of view, but it is weakened by continual internal strife, and too much attention is given over to doctrinal bickering. This is particularly true in its newsletter or quasi-magazine called the *Green Egg*. Of late, the *Green Egg* has become a forum for other Pagan groups as well, who use it for their announcements and also to air conflicting views on anything from Pagan concepts to personal behavior of their membership. The guiding force behind the Church of All Worlds and the *Green Egg* is Tim Zell, a bearded, tall, modest young man of about thirty, who states his qualifications and titles as follows:

Primate, Church of All Worlds
High Priest, Seventh Circle
CAW Central Nest
Initiate of Isis
Church of the Eternal Source
Summoner, Coven of Gwynvyd
Initiate, Delphian Coven
Charter Member, Council of American Witches

Charter Member, Nemeton
Co-founder, Council of Themis
Co-founder, Council of Earth Religions
Editor, *Green Egg*
Associate Editor, *The Pagan!*
Third Temple Degree, Rosecrucian
Graduate, Silva Mind Control
Member, Metaphysical Research Associates
Social Psychologist, Author, Artist, Lecturer, Minister,
    Life-Science Church
Minister, Church of Universal Brotherhood
Minister, Omniune Church
Pope, Paratheo-Anametamystichood of Eris Esoteric,
    Bavarian Illuminatus
Water Brother of Atel
Citizen of the Galaxie, etc.

Those wishing to subscribe to the *Green Egg,* or to learn
more about the Church of All Worlds (if you haven't already
learned about it from *The Witchcraft Report*) may write to:
Post Office Box 2953, St. Louis, Missouri 63130. Telephone:
314-725-6164. **No comment.**

Joseph Wilson, formerly of Kansas, a little later of England,
and now of St. Louis, Missouri, has his own coven, called the
Gliocas Tuatha, and those wishing to contact him may do so
by writing: Post Office Box 3840, St. Louis, Missouri 63122.
No comment.

Rarely has any activity caused as much commotion in the
occult field as the School of Wicca maintained by Gavin and
Yvonne Frost of St. Louis, Missouri. In addition to maintaining a mail-order course in witchcraft, the Frosts have also
written a book called *The Witch's Bible* and are public
lecturers on various aspects of their particular beliefs. Some
of these beliefs include sexual aspects, and on the whole differ
widely from accepted forms of Wicca. But even their most

ferocious critics acknowledge that the Frosts practice a form
of earth religion, and as such are entitled to do their thing, so
long as it harms no one. The Frosts have been called all sorts
of names and have been the subject of much criticism from
organized Paganism. Nevertheless, the Frosts maintain that
their teachings are valid and continue to run the School of
Wicca as they have for the past few years. The Frosts claim
Welsh background and a home coven in Wales itself after
which they have named their private coven. One of their
pupils, a serviceman aboard a United States ship, thanked me
for having published the address of the School of Wicca. "The
church and school has taken me off the everturning wheel and
put me on the upwards spiralling path of gnosis. For this I am
deeply grateful." Those who are interested in a mail-order
course in witchcraft may find the School of Wicca at: Route 2,
Salem, Missouri 65560. **Satisfactory.**

New Hampshire

Dr. Raymond Buckland, formerly director of the Buckland
Museum of Witchcraft and Magick at Brentwood, New York,
has moved to New Hampshire and taken his museum with
him. Along with a new wife, he has a new outlook on witchcraft, called Seax-Wica or Tradition of Saxon Witchcraft.
Founded by Ray with his wife Joan, the first rites were held on
Halloween in 1973. Dr. Buckland explains: "The need for a
new tradition was felt for many reasons, not the least being
the continual bickering and conflict found between and even
within other traditions. The primary source of this conflict
seems to be the hierarchical system, which led to severe cases
of egoism and egotism. With this in mind the Seax-Wica was
specifically designed to make such ego-trips impossible." The
complete book of Saxon Witchcraft, *The Tree,* is in the process of publication. Ancient Saxon terms are used for the
gods, goddesses, and witches. There are no degrees of ad-
vancement, and instead of the traditional dagger called

Athame, Saxon witches would carry a Seax or short dagger.
Buckland's new book will contain all the rites, rituals, prayers,
chants, etc. Dr. Buckland is a direct disciple of the late Gerald
Gardner of the Isle of Man. He is an extremely knowledgeable, sincere practitioner of witchcraft, whose reputation
should be enhanced by this latest development. Those wishing
to contact the New Hampshire coven of Dr. Raymond
Buckland may contact him at: Post Office Box 238, Weirs
Beach, New Hampshire 03246. **Recommended.**

New York

In upstate New York, there are two covens practicing Wicca,
for those who live in the area. Don F. Sawyer, of the
Atlantican Wicca, may be reached at: Liverpool, New York
13088. **No comment.**

At Watertown near the Canadian border, the Aquarian
family of covens conducts a busy and constructive occult program. In addition to the coven itself, there is now an occult
shop connected with the coven. The Aquarian Family of
covens is a fairy faith Wiccan clan, home-based in upstate New
York, having a school for students both in the area and also by
mail to other areas. The high priestess and leader, Gael Steele,
says: "Students are accepted on approval first of the *Tiphaine*
and *Dagea* of the clan, and later by the clan itself. The criteria
include seriousness and sincerity as well as the ability to come
to the mother house for initiation. For local people, lessons are
held at the mother house. The mother coven is an organization
of priests dedicated to the education of the public and interested in research into the origins of mankind, including Moo
and Atlantis, as well as the fairy faith of Great Britain
itself."

The high priestess or Tiphaine, whose cult name is Dea, is
descended from the Fairy people of France on her mother's
side and from the Clan McKenna on her father's side.

The degrees in Wicca, among the Aquarian Clan, number nine, three for each of the usual degrees of priesthood. They include three degrees of basic witchcraft, three of mystic training, psychism, and the use of the tarot deck and astrology. "As with many other groups, we do not allow the use of drugs or indulgence in homosexuality since we feel it is detrimental to the training. We also have a mail and phone order shop called 'Aquarius.' We have our own fairy amulets and talismans ranging in price from $5.00 to $100.00, robes and capes, both plain and embroidered or beaded, breech clouts to match robes, chalices, athames, bracelets, collars and necklaces. We also have both perfume and rubbing oils compounded from fairy direction and astral candles."

Those wishing to contact the shop, as well as those who want information about the coven, may address themselves to: The Aquarian Family, 802 Holcomb Street, Watertown, New York 13601. Telephone: 315-788-8947, after 11:00 A.M. and before 11:00 P.M. only. **Recommended.**

A certain Phoenix who has not risen out of any ashes, but is the high priest of the Long Island coven, also publishes an insert in the *Green Egg* called "Gardnerian Aspects," the newsletter of the Gardnerian tradition. This Long Island coven is the successor to Raymond Buckland's former group, which became Lady Rowan's group after their divorce. This coven used to be known for the long waiting periods it required of applicants, sometimes purely on whimsical grounds. Phoenix no more speaks for the entire Gardnerian form of witchcraft than a Chinese laundry does for China. Those who live in Long Island and wish to explore this group, may reach them by contacting: Phoenix c/o C.R.B. Research, Post Office Box 56, Comack, New York 11725. **Not recommended.**

In Brooklyn, New York, just over the bridge from Manhattan, there is a center of witchcraft activity known as the Warlock Shop. The Warlock Shop is the commercial division selling all sorts of goodies to the seeker, initiate, or novice. The two young men running it, Herman Slater and Ed Buczynski, also head a coven of the Welsh tradition, although neither of them is even remotely Welsh. I have detailed the nature of their coven in *The Witchcraft Report*; suffice it to say here that they are not looking for new converts but accept those they feel qualified and compatible with their particular brand of witchcraft. Both Herman and Ed have been at great pains to make homosexuality acceptable in covens that thus far have resisted it on a number of weighty grounds. Recently, they have started to publish an interesting newspaper called the *Earth Religion News*, which contains a great deal of information as well as breezy gossip so dear to the hearts of the average Pagan. It also contains an amazing amount of paid advertising, witness to the enterprising spirit of the two young men. Make no mistake about it, Herman and Ed have made witchcraft pay, and what they have started as a sideline has become a solid major occupation for them. Each issue of the *Earth Religion News* seems to be an improvement on the previous one, which is a happy thought indeed. Lately, the *Earth Religion News* has begun to expose outright phonies in the Pagan movement, such as the great "Druid" of Philadelphia, about whom I had written similarly about a year before they did. The paper claims to be completely non-sectarian at all times, and this must be true, because they are even printing advertising matter from competitors—in Brooklyn yet! Even more fascinating is the catalog of the Warlock Shop. The catalog contains an incredible number of articles, some of which are connected with the occult, while others merely fit into the general mood. Anyone who cannot find everything he needs for his particular coven or witchcraft activities in this catalog simply doesn't know what it is all about. Among other things, there are replicas of classical statuary. Not all descriptions are correct, but the prices are reasonable.

Lately, Herman and Ed have renamed their coven the New York coven, even though they are located in downtown Brooklyn, but as long as there is no Manhattan coven to dispute it, I suppose the title is all right. Those wishing to get to know the two fellows and their amazing array of merchandise, or find out about their covenstead and its secrets, may wish to drop in on them at: 300 Henry Street, Brooklyn, New York 11201. Telephone: 212-625-9001. **No comment.**

In New York City itself, Dr. Leo Louis Matello has become somewhat of an institution, a one-man establishment fighting the cause of witchcraft, taking on anyone and everyone who dares dispute him. Among the "organizations" this fiery Sicilian has created is "The Witches' Anti-defamation League (later copied by Isaac Bonevits under the title of Aquarian Anti-defamation League), the Witches' Liberation Movement, and even The Witches' Encounter Bureau, for witches in need of company. He edits the *Wicca Newsletter* and *Witchcraft Digest* and has written numerous books, the latest being, *Witchcraft: The Old Religion.* It is a valuable compendium of the traditions and inner workings of the craft. Martello has been initiated into four other traditions besides his own Sicilian one, and in 1971 won the first civil rights victory for witches when he threatened to sue the New York Parks Department for religious discrimination, when they refused him a permit for his "witch-in." Make no mistake about it, Martello's militant, strident voice, wild hairdo and beard do not go down well with establishment types—but his heart is in his work. He has been a professional graphologist for twenty-five years, and in now in his early forties. Because of the demands on his time, he had his phone disconnected and is somewhat of a recluse living with a group of dogs. Lately, Martello has begun to advertise a mail-order witchcraft course, whereby applicants may receive their lessons in order to qualify as witches later on. He also maintains a healing registry, using a Tibetan prayer wheel to help people in distress. He says about himself, "though I make no claim, promise nothing, my files are full of testimonial letters from people who have benefitted from this free service." He also offers absent or distant exorcism for those in need of this particular service. In the many disputes now tearing the Pagan movement asunder, one never knows which side Martello is on at any given moment; but one thing is certain, whichever side he is on, he will fight like nobody's business. Those interested in acquiring some of Martello's own books, or others he handles, or the newsletter, or just Martello himself, may write to: Dr. Leo Louis Martello, Suite 1B, 153 West Eightieth Street, New York, New York 10034. **Satisfactory.**

Ohio

There is hardly a more charming witch in Toledo than Circe, a lady who also runs an occult supply shop, teaches witchcraft and other pursuits, and maintains an open house to those seeking enlightenment in the Pagan religion. Circe may be reached at: 2242 Parkwood, Toledo, Ohio 43620. **Recommended.**

Enchanted Herbs produces and sells unusual occult and health herbal products. The pure and organic ingredients are grown, gathered, and prepared by Selene, a solitary witch who lives in a rural area of northeastern Ohio. You may write for details to: Enchanted Herbs, 12099 County Line Road, Chesterland, Ohio 44026. **Recommended.**

In *The New Pagans*, I spoke of a "good Satanist" by the name of Dr. Herbert Sloane, an older gentleman who was once a barber but who has become a professional card reader for the past ten or more years. Herb Sloane is also the head of a little group calling itself "Our Lady of Endor Coven of the Ophite Gnostic Cultus Sathanas." His brand of Satanism differs greatly from that practiced by Anton LaVey and is really nothing more than a Methodist service in which Lord

Sathanas is substituted for the Lord or Jesus Christ. This coven fits the midwestern mood, worships in street clothes, although the high priest does put a pair of plastic horns onto his forehead during the service. Those who would like to know more about Herb Sloane's Satanism may find him at: 808 West Central Avenue, Toledo, Ohio 43610. **No comment.**

Even in staid Columbus, there is an active Satanist group. This one used to be in the Dayton, Ohio area, but its high priest and leader, John De Haven, a sometime radio personality and writer, has moved to Columbus, so the group has changed headquarters. The Church of Satanic Brotherhood has an active program of meetings, initiations, and rituals, some of which have most poetic names: Ritual of the Stifling Air, Initiation of New Members and General Lust Ritual, and Ritual of Christian Madness. There are overtones of a college fraternity in some of these proceedings, but John De Haven and his friends do maintain a lively correspondence among themselves and with others, explaining their point of view, and fighting Anton LaVey. "God is not dead, man *is* God," reads one of the articles in their newsletter. "Man is the absolute monarch, man alone possesses the seed of life and his flesh proclaims his divine nature. Man proposes and disposes, according to his will, and allows himself to become subjective only when such subjection coincides with the means to continue along his path. If changes must be made, then it is man who makes them."

There is nothing particularly diabolical about this group, membership is mainly among young people, and those who wish to learn more about their particular philosophy, may write to: The Church of Satanic Brotherhood, Post Office Box 325, Columbus—Worthington, Ohio 43085. **No comment.**

Oklahoma

Until very recently, Joseph Ferrante, a young man with deep interests in witchcraft, maintained a small coven in the Lawton area. For some time, he had published a local newsletter, but he found himself the innocent butt of a controversy between rival witches. He prefers to go underground, therefore, and canceled all preparations already made for the resumption of a newsletter that was to be called "The Night Owl." Although Mr. Ferrante no longer seeks contacts in this area, as an individual he is recommended.

Oregon

Sara Cunningham has recently established a rural covenstead, moving to Oregon from her busy house in Pasadena, California. Here she will teach, write, and produce the unique oils, herbs, and incenses that have made her justly famous. "I am truly at home here in the forest," she says. "I think my Druidic ancestry has come to fruition here, and the Sacred Oak Grove has such power that it chills the very marrow in my bones."

Sara is a tall, red-headed young woman of New England background who has been teaching Celtic witchcraft for many years. At one time, she and the aforementioned Harold Moss were involved with an Egyptian church in Pasadena, California, but the partnership did not last very long, due to conflicting interests. For the present, Sara Cunningham has closed her shop in Pasadena, Stonehenge, on Green Street, but eventually she hopes to use her Oregon headquarters as the point of supply. Those wishing to find out about possible classes as well as products may write to: Lady Sara, Post Office Box 204, Wolf Creek, Oregon 97497. Her covenstead is registered under the name of First Temple of Tiphareth. All occult supplies can be obtained from the Oregon address. Telephone: 213-795-4570. **Recommended.**

Pennsylvania

The Crystal Well is the new name for what began as the

Waxing Moon under Joseph Wilson, but is now published by Thomas, no last name, at Post Office Box 18351, Philadelphia, Pennsylvania 19120. There is no subscription however, and donations are accepted by the publisher. Thomas calls it "the oldest continuously published newsletter concerning witchcraft in the United States." Beautifully illustrated, this is an attractive publication worthy of any seeker in witchcraft. Undoubtedly, those wishing information concerning a coven in Pennsylvania may find Thomas helpful.

Texas

Dallas has one of the finest Pagan groups in the country, a Dianic witchcraft coven, headed by Morgan, with the assistance of her life-mate, Mark Roberts. Both Morgan and Mark lead useful lives in the professions, he in television, and she in teaching, and their house is a model of warm, artistic living. In addition, Mr. Roberts publishes *The New Broom*, a journal of witchcraft, which contains much useful material. The coven classes itself as Dianic, in the sense that it recognizes the parthenogenetic birth of the goddess, very much the way Jesus Christ was conceived without benefit of earthly father. In this respect, the Dallas coven follows perhaps the purest form of Wicca, but in removing the need for the Horned God, the companion of Diana, they are by no means slighting the role of male witches. The group numbers some twenty or thirty, the majority in the Outer Court waiting to ascend the ladder to full initiation. Coven, magazine, and people of the Dallas group are of the highest order. There are also twenty-seven "groves" or branches scattered throughout the United States. Those wishing to make contact should write to: *The New Broom*, Post Office Box 1646, Dallas, Texas 75221. **Recommended.**

In Houston, Don C. Overstreet, a former psychic healer and medium, now runs a Celtic Order of Wicca, teaching and initiating those who would want to become witches. Those interested in Wicca in the Houston area may contact Mr. Overstreet at: 6019 Camellia, Houston, Texas 77007. **Satisfactory.**

Virginia

At Hampton, Virginia, a new periodical called simply *X* is being published by Rod Frye, an enthusiastic young man bent on propagating occult and Pagan information. Those living in the Virginia area might query him for possible coven activities. Address: Post Office Box 7374, Hampton, Virginia 23366. **Satisfactory.**

West Virginia

An astrologer and "professional witch" by the name of Merlin Magus, with a sense of humor, runs a small coven called the Universal Church of Wicca at Princeton, West Virginia. Merlin Magus's worldly name is Hansel Tabor. His "rituals," however, are erotic fantasies. Those who wish to contact Mr. Tabor nevertheless will find him at: Universal Church of Wicca, Post Office Box 1102, Princeton, West Virginia 24740. **Not recommended.**

Wyoming

Although I know of no particular accomplishment by this coven, I wish to list the Delphian Coven, headed by one Bonnie Sherlock, who appears from time to time in the pages of the *Green Egg*, commenting or complaining about this and that. Bonnie Sherlock may be reached at: Box 48, Route 62, Lander, Wyoming 82520. **No comment.**

Canada

Those seeking a group in Canada may wish to correspond with Roy Dymond, Box 715, Stouffville, Ontario. Mr. Dymond, who owns a health shop and is a professional masseur, is very knowledgeable about craft activities.

In Toronto, Carole Ramsbottom heads a small Wicca coven, following the Gardnerian ritual, although several members are hereditary witches. Those who live in and around Toronto, may wish to write to Carol Ramsbottom at: 10 Winter Avenue, Scarborough, Ontario, Canada. **Recommended.**

Recently, some of the Pagan leaders who have been criticized for their bickering and extreme criticism of others in the movement proclaimed their intention of writing their own books, thus freeing them from external pressures. To that end, a questionnaire has recently been sent to many active in the Pagan field, in which they are being asked all sorts of questions about their activities, personal status, and other pertinent information, in order to enable Mr. and Mrs. Tim Zell, editors of the *Green Egg*, to write that promised book.

Although I am extremely respectful of genuine Pagan activities and consider witchcraft a valid religious expression, I find the infighting among a small but vociferous segment of the Pagan community disturbing. At a time when Pagans as a religious organization are just beginning to be taken seriously by society, and when being a witch is not followed by exclamations of horror or disbelief (or suggestions to consult a psychiatrist), the excesses and fantasies of a few minority leaders among witches and Pagans in general, tend to retard if not undo the progress the movement has made.

Those who are interested in witchcraft and the Pagan movement in general, may wish to read other books in addition to my own, of course. I particularly recommend the books written by Sybil Leek, Doreen Valiente, Leo Martello, Stewart Farrar's *What Witches Do*, Gerald Gardner, Robert Graves, and Paul Husson. Most of the periodicals now extant I have already mentioned with their respective publishers, frequently also the heads of the local coven. The *Pentagram*, which was published in England for some time, does not appear any longer.

9

An Occult ABC

Most laymen, even some "believers," are confused concerning the true meaning of terms frequently used in the occult field. Others do not fully understand the differences between certain terms, such as ESP and parapsychology, medium and clairvoyant, and so on. For that reason, I have selected the *most commonly used* terms and arranged alphabetical explanations for them. Those looking for more sophisticated *termini technici*, such as some of the East Indian words used in meditation, can find them in books specializing in the respective subdivisions. For the average reader, the following glossary should prove sufficient and helpful.

Some of my explanations may differ from those listed in other sources, especially general encyclopedias or dictionaries. It should be remembered that such general works are not geared to the occult field per se and may contain misinformation or false definitions. Many recent editions of general encylopedias have, for instance, begun to redefine their explanations of witchcraft, seances, and other basic terms to bring them more in line with current thinking.

Astral Projection

Also called "out of the body experience," it refers to the sensation of leaving the physical body, traveling at great speed to distant places, and observing various events, people, and situations. Upon return to the body, usually a sensation of falling from great heights is present, as the traveling speed of the "inner" or spiritual body is sharply reduced to fit it back into place within the slower, denser physical body. Subjects usually recall their "trip" in great detail. Astral projection can also be experimentally induced under test conditions. It is totally different from ordinary dreams in that it is a clear, precise memory of having been places. Some astral travelers are physically tired as if they had really traveled about.

Black Mass

Essentially the product of the bored upper strata of British and French society during the second half of the eighteenth century, the ceremony harks back to the Middle Ages where it was practiced on rare occasions by anticlerical elements, and sometimes by individuals seeking power through it. During the eighteenth century, it was a fashionable thrill. It is rarely practiced today, except by individuals and groups on the fringes of mental aberration.

It consists of a deliberate reversal of the Roman Catholic Mass, from the cross being hung upside down to the litany being said backwards. The Black Mass is thought to mock God and Jesus Christ. Witches never practice Black Masses simply because they do not accept the existence of the Christian religion. They will not mock that which did not exist at the time their cult came into being, thousands of years before Christianity.

Clairvoyance, Clairaudience, Clairsentience

The ability to see, hear, or smell beyond the ordinary five senses. A clairvoyant person foresees events before they happen, or while they happen at a distance from the clairvoyant's location. Seeing into the past is also part of this gift, as is the ability to see, hear, or smell events, people, and things not physically present but existing either in another place or on another plane of existence, such as the so-called "hereafter."

Control Personality

Trance mediums have guides, sometimes called controls or control personalities. These are individuals who have died and then attached themselves to the particular medium to help her or him. Their role is much like that of a telephone operator between worlds. Some psychiatrists feel that the controls are in reality split-off parts of the medium's own personality. However, some parapsychologists do accept the individual existence of the controls as independent persons, especially in cases in which the control shows marked personality differences from the medium's own.

Déjà Vu

Literally "already seen," the term means the sudden, fleeting impression many people have of having been to a place, having met someone before, or having heard, seen, or done something before, which in reality they have not. For example, a soldier going overseas for the first time might recognize a certain house in a strange city as if he had been there before. Or a person might hear himself say something he knows he has said in exactly the same words before but cannot recall when.

The overwhelming number of these déjà vu flashes must be explained as precognitive flashes (*see* Precognition), that is to say, foreknowledge of the event experienced prior to the actual occurrence, but unnoticed by the person having the experience at that time. However, when the event becomes "objective reality," the fact that one is familiar with the event is realized and the precognitive flash acknowledged. A smaller percentage of déjà vu experiences, however, clearly indicate partial reincarnation memories.

Dreams

There are four types of dreams: dreams caused by physical stress, such as indigestion; dreams of psychoanalytical nature expressing suppressed emotions or desires; astral projection dreams (see Astral Projection); and psychic or true dreams. In the latter, the sleeper receives specific information about the future, either in the form of a warning of events to come or in the form of a scene showing the event as inevitable. Sometimes deceased individuals make contact with the sleeper in this state when his resistance to receiving communication from the beyond is lower than while fully awake.

Ectoplasm

Examined some years ago at the University of London, ectoplasm turned out to be an albumen substance related to the sexual fluids within the body and secreted by certain glands. It is present during so-called materialization seances (see Materialization) and in thinner form also when apparitions occur, as well as in poltergeist (see Poltergeist) phenomena when ectoplasm is formed to move physical objects about. It comes from inside the body of the medium as well as the sitters (see Medium and Sitting), and it must be returned after the experiment to avoid damage to the health of the individuals. Ectoplasm is sensitive to white and yellow light and can exist safely only in dark red illumination.

ESP

The term was coined by Dr. Joseph B. Rhine, formerly of Duke University. Extrasensory perception, in my definition, is the obtaining of information beyond that possible by ordinary means and the five senses as we know them today. It operates through the so-called sixth sense. The latter is not a separate sense but merely the extension of the five senses beyond what we ordinarily think are their limitations, but which in fact, are not.

Neither extrasensory perception nor the sixth sense imply anthing supernatural.

Ether and Etheric Body

The ether in this context is the surrounding atmosphere in the sense that it conducts psychic emanations. Thoughts travel through the ether, and apparitions of the dead exist in the etheric world. The etheric body is the finer, inner body, an exact duplicate of the grosser, outer or physical body. At death, the etheric body assumes all functions and appearances of the physical shell.

Ghost

Ghosts are the surviving emotional memories of people who have died violently, or in some way traumatically, and who cannot leave the place of their unexpected or untimely passing. Ghosts are people with their mental faculties severely curtailed, limited to their last impulses, such as some unfinished business or complaint, and they are often unaware of their true status, that is, being outside a physical body. Ghosts neither travel from place to place nor do they normally harm anyone except through fear. The latter is unwarranted since ghosts are entirely occupied with their own problems. These visual images of dead people have been photographed under satisfactory scientific test conditions.

Glossalalia

Also called "speaking with tongues" by religiously oriented researchers, this is nothing more than the ability of trance.

The voice speaking through the entranced person may speak in a language totally unknown to the speaker while in his or her conscious state, or it may even be a fantasy language.

Hypnosis

The state of detachment from the conscious self induced by verbal commands or other means, such as sound and light patterns, in which the subject will do two things: (1) reveal freely his innermost thoughts beyond what he will reveal in the conscious state for various reasons; and (2) accept suggestions he must carry out after he is returned to the normal state. Hypnosis is safe in the hands of medical doctors and of trained psychic researchers when it is also used in reincarnation experiments (see Regression). It is not a stage entertainment, although often used as such, and even less of a parlor game.

Incantation

In the Pagan cults, especially witchcraft, incantations are intense emotional appeals to the deity to do certain things for the petitioner. They are similar to prayers except that they are not dependent on the goodwill of the deity. Incantations always work, in the view of the Pagan believer, because they contain just the right formula, just the proper words to "make things happen."

Karma

Not merely an East Indian religious philosophy, but part of the system of reincarnation accepted equally by many in the Western world, karma is the universal law of rewards for certain actions undertaken in one lifetime but paid off in another. The individual does not generally know what his or her karma from the past consists of; the karmic law operates in the way certain opportunities arise in the present life, or in the way people meet again who may have known each other in an earlier life. What the individual does of his own free will, and from his own moral and spiritual resources, will determine the manner in which the karma is "paid off" or extinguished.

Levitation

The ability, often photographed, of physical objects, such as tables and chairs and occasionally even people, to float above the floor for a short time. This is caused by an electromagnetic force field created through the body of a powerful "physical" medium in the immediate vicinity. Great religious ecstasy has on occasion also lowered the weight of a person temporarily so that he would "float up" to the ceiling. It cannot be reproduced at will, however.

Magic(k)

The practical "arm" of witchcraft and other Pagan cults, magic, sometimes spelled with a *k* in the antiquated fashion to distinguish it from modern stage magic with which it has nothing in common, is the better and deeper understanding of the laws of nature beyond that which the average person knows. In this knowledge lie answers to manipulating certain events and people that seem miraculous but are, in effect, perfectly natural.

Materialization

The rare and often imitated ability of producing ectoplasm, which in turn takes on the actual three-dimensional forms of deceased persons. Genuine materialization experiments have been conducted in England by reputable researchers, usually in rooms illuminated by adequate red light. The materialization medium usually sits in a black "cabinet" or closet, open on one side only, and the ectoplasm pours from the mouth and nose of the deeply entranced medium. Genuine materializations rise slowly from the floor and eventually melt back into it when the power fails. Counterfeit materializations, such as have been staged for years in American Spiritualist camps in the summer months, can be spotted fairly easily since the materialized "spirit" forms walk on and off in their full heights.

Medium

A much misunderstood term, medium means intermediary, that is to say a channel between the world of the living and the world of the dead, but it also means a person able to foretell future events and sometimes read the unknown past (*see also* Psychic). Mental mediumship includes clairvoyance, clairaudience, clairsentience, and psychometry, while physical mediumship (much rarer) consists of trance and materialization (*see under those headings*). Mediums never "summon" anyone; they merely relate what communications they receive to their clients.

Poltergeist

Formerly thought to be the product of unused sexual energies in pubescent young adults, who cause objects to fly about in destructive ways to attract attention to themselves, the phenomena now are thought by others, including myself, to be part of ghostly manifestations. However, the unused powers of pubescent youngsters, or sometimes of retarded older people, are used by outside forces, generally deceased individuals bent on making their continued presences felt, sometimes in a malevolent fashion.

Precognition

The ability to know ahead of time events transpiring at a later date, or to know something happening a distance away without recourse to the ordinary five senses or any foreknowledge whatever, either consciously or unconsciously.

Premonition

A vague feeling of impending events, usually destructive, sometimes specific in details, more often a general misgiving that something bad will be happening to someone, including oneself.

Psychic

The term psychic refers to the broad spectrum of all ESP phenomena, anything transcending the ordinary five senses; a psychic is a medium.

Psychometry

The fairly common ability to "read" past, present, or future events involving a person by touching an object owned by that person, preferably something that person alone has owned, and worn on the person, such as a ring, a comb, or a watch. Emotional stimuli coat the object the way a thin coat of silver salts coats a photographic plate. Sensitives can reconstruct the events or read them in the future from the touch of the object.

Regression

Hypnotic regression, undertaken by qualified researchers, takes the subject in stages to his or her childhood and then cautiously past birth into an assumed earlier life. The majority of people do not recall any previous incarnation under hypnotic regression even if they consciously would like to.

A few are given to fantasizing to please the hypnotist and will create "lives" in the past. An impressive if small number of individuals have been regressed and found to have had evidential information about previous lives buried deep in their unconscious minds. All of these subjects, however, have had conscious, waking flashes of having been someone else before and were regressed only to deepen the memory of a previous incarnation, and not to find it.

Reincarnation

The conscious existence in another body and as another person, whether male or female, in a lifetime on earth prior to the present one, and the assumed continuance of that process into another life after the current reincarnation. I have documented several verified cases in *Born Again*, and Dr. Ian Stevenson has done likewise in *Twenty Cases Suggestive of Reincarnation*. Reincarnation works for everybody, but only a few can recall their previous lives, notably those whose lives were cut short for one reason or another.

Satanism

The cult of worshiping the devil principle, that is to say, human selfishness, greed, lust, and self-satisfaction. Modern Satanists, such as Anton LaVey of San Francisco's First Church of Satan, do not deny the existence of the spiritual element in man, nor the survival of human personality after death. They teach full enjoyment of the physical self, however, and are firmly opposed to charity, compassion, and other unselfish traits. True Satanists, such as exist here and there, are on the fringes of the law and sometimes involve themselves in ritual killings, usually, but not exclusively, of animals. Satanists and devil worshipers have nothing to do with witchcraft, even though they are often confused in the popular mind. Witches and Satanists are in fact opposites.

Seance

Actually the word means "sitting down" and refers to the assembly of several people for the purpose of spirit communication, psychic development, or other ESP research on a personal basis. Spiritualist seances often involve the holding of hands to create a "circle of power" for a few moments, or the singing of religious hymns to raise the "vibrations" (*see* Vibrations). Seances can take place in the daytime or at night and are usually held in subdued light. Only in materialization seances do "spirits" appear or objects move. The majority of seances is for verbal communication only, through the mouth of the medium at the head of the table.

Sensitive

The same as medium or being a psychic.

Sitting and Sitter

Sitting is a more appropriate term for seance, and a sitter is a person taking part in a sitting, or someone consulting a medium privately and individually.

Spell

A spell is a prayer with the force of a directive used in witchcraft and other Pagan cults to make certain things happen to another person not present when the spell is cast. The specific choice of words, certain ritual actions, and other aids are required to make the spell effective.

Spirit

The "inner self," that which survives physical death of the body. The spirit must not be confused with a ghost, which is an earth-bound spirit unable to move on into what Dr. Joseph B. Rhine has called the world of the mind. Spirits are free to come and go; they inhabit the world next to ours in which thoughts are instant action. Spirits are electromagnetic fields formed in the exact duplicate of the person's physical self prior to death, but usually returned to his or her prime state. Thus spirits, when they appear to the living, usually show themselves in their best years, although they are able to control their appearances at will, being thought forms only.

Spiritualism

A religion of Christian moral based upon the findings of psychic research and the belief in continuance of life in "summerland." Founded in the 1860s in America and popular also in Great Britain, Spiritualism still flourishes in many subdivisions and sects and is a recognized form of religion. It should not be confused with psychic research or parapsychology, however.

Telekinesis and Teleportation

The movement of solid objects by power of mind. This has been done in laboratory experiments at Duke University and recently in Soviet Russia, where it was also recorded photographically. The energy streaming out of the medium's body causes the objects to move. Teleportation is much rarer and less well documented. It involves the sudden and dramatic transportation of solid objects great distances and sometimes *through* solid objects, utilizing techniques of dematerialization and rematerialization not yet fully understood.

Trance

A state in which the medium's own personality is temporarily set aside and the spirit or personality of another person is allowed to enter the medium's body and operate the speech mechanism, vocal chords, facial muscles, etc., the way a driver operates an automobile. The driver is not the car, and the medium is not the entity speaking through her. Afterwards, the medium does not recall her actions or words while in possession by another being. Trance should only be undertaken in the presence of and under the supervision of a trained psychic researcher.

Transmigration

An East Indian belief that reincarnation is possible between humans and animals. For the present, no evidence for this exists.

Vibrations

Called "vibes" by the young, these are movements of emotionally charged particles filling the ether (*see* Ether) in which we exist. They manifest themselves as emanations, rays, impressions, electromagnetic energy patterns, and so on.

Vision

A visual experience concerning events not visible to the eye at the place and time where it occurs. Swedenborg had a vision of the Stockholm fire while a day's journey away. Some visions pertain to future events also.

Witchcraft

Anglo-Saxon/Celtic witchcraft, called "Wicca," or "craft of the wise," is also known as "the Old Religion" by its followers. It is a true nature religion based upon three important elements:

1. The firm conviction that reincarnation is a fact and that the cycle of life continues beyond death.

2. The belief in the powers of magic, the better utilization of natural law, to make certain things happen that ordinary people are unable to accomplish.

3. The worship of the "Mother Goddess" principle of a female deity, representing the creative element in nature, thus free from original sin, guilt, shame, and anything restricting oneself to the narrow limits of an artificially motivated society. "An' it harm none, do what thou wilt," is the *sole* law of Wicca.